Also by Chris Ransick

Poetry Collections

Never Summer: Poems From Thin Air
Lost Songs & Last Chances

Fiction

A Return to Emptiness

Asleep Beneath the Hill of Dreams

Poems

CHRIS RANSICK

Ghost Road Press

Ghost Road Press
Denver, Colorado
www.ghostroadpress.com

Library of Congress Cataloging-in-Publication Data.
Asleep Beneath the Hill of Dreams
Ghost Road Press
ISBN 13 digit 978-0-9825043-6-9; 10 digit 0-9825043-6-5
Library of Congress Control Number: 2009937479
Cover Photo: Shannon Skaife
Cover design and interior layout: Matthew Davis

ACKNOWLEDGMENTS

Thanks go out to the editors of the following journals who first published these poems: "Dream of Your House, Demolished" *Notre Dame Review;* "Dream of the Golf Widows" *Colorado Lawyer;* "Dream of the Dying Soldier" *The Coe Review;* "Dream of the Surgeon" *Ars Medica;* "Dream at the Intersection" *Wazee Journal.*

Thanks, always, to Dean Huffaker for his insight and care with the developing manuscript.

CONTENTS

The waking have one world
in common. Sleepers
meanwhile turn aside, each
into a darkness of his own.

Heraclitus

for Shannon
beside whom I dream

Dream of Your House, Demolished

The kitchen is the heart of the house so
it all starts there, a disassembly of every meal
you shared. First, the conversations
are sucked back toward silence, slowly,
so meanings can be detached word by word
to assure understanding is erased. Libations
flow back into decanters, though wine
will never become again sweet grapes
nor lamb find hooves, though it uncooks
and returns to raw flesh sealed in plastic.
Peppers, onions, red tomatoes rise from
deep dishes and form bulbs again,
then roll out toward their garden stalks.
The living room is next and takes less time.
Sofa that absorbed your many naps uncradles
dreams and snores almost melodious
rippling backward. In the bathroom,
dirt and suds ooze up from drains.
The mirror plays a movie of faces, each
staring until self-awareness retreats and
disappears into a look of longing.
In your old bedroom, a lack of love
moves gradually beneath the sheets toward
love again, more vigorous with each
passing night. Erolalia sounds the same
returning as emerging. When finally,
each visitor who once was welcomed is
sent away a stranger again, you arrive
at the first time you saw the place. That vision
fades back into its seam. The bulldozer comes,
the dump trucks and the anti-carpenters.
Their business is with timber and brick
which now, unhoused, will yield.

Dream at the High School Graduation

June sun glints off the heads of fathers
huddled on bleachers, bad backs aching
where gone wings were, the phantom limbs
of amputees. Sons' and daughters' robes
glow blue enough to be criminal under
such skies. Far figures lift off artificial turf
in effortless flight. You see no chorus, though voices
drift in harmonies once thought theoretical,
a song not written, one you'll never hear again.
The great mass of diplomas stacked stage left
surges up like a tsunami, crashes down to
swallow the principal who outlawed dissent,
even as she made it necessary. Who will
replace the rebel child in your house, she who
departs this green ritual a new priestess
heading for a town with no temple?
Bells ring in bell towers you built but
the congregation is now mostly mirrors
propped in chairs. Ancient cottonwoods
shading the perimeter denude themselves
when the graduates march beneath, revealing
a truth you must relearn: seasons circle,
never change. Only the guest list shifts.
How will you ever walk past this field
in winter and not weep when the moon
slides out from a cloud to paint these
remembered shapes, platinum on a
black canvas? Such worries, coined in a
dream, can't be spent in waking worlds.
Move now among these heirs to your
poor fortune of good wine and gardens,
and twist once more their jade tendrils,
reaching and reaching, round the trellis.

Dream of the Author

You wake before dawn, the last blacks of night
greying with something less than light, the air
stirred by wind, your muse suspended by her
lovely ankles from a cottonwood's thickest
branch. Somewhere down the block a black dog
barks at invisible men. As you lie there listening
and the cur's frantic snarls form a phrase
you recognize, the first sentence of your
unwritten masterpiece, a gold-threaded hem
which receded from your fingers the more
desperately you reached. In the next room,
your keyboard clacks, but whose hands
are dancing there—not yours. You rise,
hurry in to find the many pages produced
yesterday are gone. In their place are
slices of cheese, one sticking a pale tongue
out of the stack. The doorbell rings
and you open the door to see the mailman
fleeing, jettisoning his bag of junkmail.
The package he left has burst its wrap
and drips blood onto the step. You find
inside the hideous cover your publisher
will choose for your next book. Hands
tap at your keyboard again and
you decide to let them go, sure the lexicon
of ghosts will exceed in style your own.
When you return to bed only to find
you're now the only customer in a
failing bookstore, the afternoon so quiet
you hear the shelved books murmuring
favorite passages, pages straining to
escape their bindings, the ink running
as though words came cheap. The first tome
you open snaps shut again as if you'd

revealed its inner nakedness. The next releases
a flock of swallows. Another erupts in an
operatic aria. A thin volume of poems
melts in your hands, its residue
black phrases the poet excised. The clerk
watches your every move, follows to
wipe your fingerprints from spines. You find
no books you wish to buy, not even your own.

Dream at Summer's End

The creek rises during the night, floods your bedroom
so you wake afloat, moving down gentle currents, nudged
by soft branches that stroke skin. You bump against
mossy rocks, your nostrils full of mudscent, tickled by
waterskeeters and the fleshy whiskers of carp.
Two stars burn white on the western horizon, fade
as inky dawn turns powder-blue, crescent moon's
tips tilted to cup what it can of liquid sky.
You'd like to stay, rolling in your buoyant bodyboat,
hoping silence might encourage your black brethren,
the crows, to stay on their perches high in the spruce,
cawing complaints about mortality—or are their
harsh calls for you? Glossy leaves spill down the
garden trellis, a dense green refuge where bees intone,
reminding you of another summer when you ran
all day in grassy fields, tumbled down embankments,
hunted in brambles that scribed your calves and
sunburnt cheeks with red runes, the language of boys
blackberry filled, who climbed on maple parapets.
Garter snakes slip through tall grass, whisper *autumn*
as though you will not notice what they say,
but at the sound, tufts fly loose from Canadian thistles
and rabbits in burrows tremble to think of the fox.
Heatwaves hover above black pavement, but that
won't last. Soon enough, the laggard sun will slide low
and the few women left in town will shapeshift into
elegant geese and fly south. Everywhere you look
surrender begins and though it's sadder than seeing
Ophelia in the stream, you decide to watch it all,
even the vine abandoning tendrils as yet unattached,
the better to rattle dangling seedpods, its last chance.

Dream on a Foreign Street

You wake on a bridge across a turgid river
amid people speaking five strange tongues,
each asking directions as if you were
local, as if your shoes knew these cobbles well,
as if you could turn down a narrow lane
and point out the place of your birth. You shrug
and point toward the far bank. They misunderstand
and begin to strip off their clothes, dive
down through the floating garbage, swim for the
shore. Somewhere, an orchestra plays
furiously, the music summoning sheets of rain
from the sky. Inside a store, you find boxes of
bread so dark, night falls when you eat.
The man at the counter wants coins
minted in some other land. Give me, he says,
both your thumbs instead and I will
make change. You run away and mongrel dogs
chase you down spiral stairs. Underground,
the walls are moist and you navigate
by the light of a torch. Trains run heavily
overhead and a frightened woman
hurries past, pursued by shadows.
You emerge in the bleached rotunda of a great
museum. Everywhere you look, urns behind glass
totter at the edge of history, threatening to spill
truths. A uniformed man watches you, speaks
into his radio, nods and smiles, his teeth
pointed. Soon, the museum will close. You know
because the lights are growing dim. A great
sarcophagus begins to glow, the capstone
grinding open, and out comes your first lover.
She's beckoning you. Marble statues
turn to stare and see what you will do.

Dream at the Intersection

It's unexpected, coming as it does from your
blind spot, a truck carrying buckets of paint
that clatter, spill, and splash onto
asphalt, the browns and greens and yellows
commingling with blood. The result: your demise
is a Magritte, a surreal scene, a pastiche.
Helicopters hover instantly, distant cameras
capturing the composition meant to tickle
television screens at 10 p.m.
The first thing to go is your voice so you
lie along the curb, blinking at paramedics
whose fast hands tear the plastic bags,
coiled contents springing toward your veins.
Crows come from miles away, roost
on a microwave tower, nonchalant voyeurs.
A strange woman kneels and grasps
your hand, at first a comfort until you sense
she'll never let go. Her irises turn to
rainbows circling dark stars, her message
simple: these black discs are doors.
Systole and diastole slow as though
the oarsmen of your boat approach the dock.
A numb foot claims an ankle, then a knee,
and fractures cease to throb. You recall
a girl you kissed by a stream, a summer night
in a life you now know was borrowed.

Five Days at the Dream Job

Monday

Four friendly dogs lope down a great lawn,
toward the forest from which you emerge,
beech and oak leaves in your hair.
A stream spills by, murmuring names
of dead scholars. You're hired in mid-interview,
then offered cold beer and pretzels.
Mephistopheles, your office mate,
tells you how he and Faust
play golf each week in Eden. Books lie open
everywhere, their pages full of poems
that break free, float through shafts of sun
all afternoon, burying the path back.

Tuesday

A crew of fairies, foul smelling and smudged,
sprawl across the piles of papers
as though waiting for pizzas to arrive.
But by morning they've managed
to grade the whole stack.

Wednesday

Every Wednesday, the building disappears.
Luckily, it only rains on Tuesdays. Professors
serve steak to custodians, who teach the classes
for a day. The students recite Keats and Shelley
and plant their little pills like seeds. No one
argues over a parking space on Wednesdays.
If you get a raise, it comes on this day.

You are complimented sincerely
for the first time since 1996, and must sit down.
The Governor, previously an asshole,
calls to say he's giving up religion and promises
the layoffs and cutbacks are over.
You have a guest for class, the ghost
of Aristotle toting his lost books,
and everyone is pleased as he begins.

Thursday

Ten years pass. Grey-tailed comets
left dust in your hair as you
slept beneath the stars. You teach your classes

in the crevasse of a glacier to slow time.
The ice is blue and clear, sun pouring
through those halls a light too pale

to melt the walls. The discussion turns to
Ophelia, and whether the cold Danish wind
made the water seem warm at the last.

Friday

It's your last day; only your closest friend
knows, and does not tell. You cancel
all assignments and the students pair off
to make love in the sun-splashed grass.
The red light on your phone blinks,
then goes out by itself. The office coffee
flows chocolate and raspberry
over your tongue and breezes
blowing through your window feather
gentle fingers across your neck.

You leave when no one is looking,
out the front door and down the sloping lawn,
toward the forest greening with May.

Dream of the Synesthete

You wake up in a bed soft as yellow,
aroma of crushed almonds wafting from the
number 6 on your alarm. Red dawn
wets drawn drapes coarse as sandstone. In your
dark dream, interrogators strained flavors from a
man's tongue, one by one. He cried for mercy
and they gave him chocolate decadence
he could not taste, though his mouth filled with
vibrations, mellifluous woodwinds,
oboes and bassoons bruising flesh.
It's a winter Tuesday, cold air so loud that
squirrels drop dead from branches
into piles of fallen leaves that sound like
musk, a smell sharp as an axe hacking
into a stump. Sweet orange juice
tastes cacophonous and scalding coffee
gutters in your mouth, a candle wick
dancing in wind. You smell the burning
too late, your body already afire,
emanating cinnamon and power chords.
Peaches hum, ripening in a bowl, and
morning tastes like a callused finger
probing your gelatinous heart. You would
like to know why the birds sing backward,
their tunes almost familiar as they reverse
between beaks. You've never been bitten
by the neighbor's dog but it barks and you
flinch, feeling cold water splash your face.
Damn that dog, damn the sun playing
arpeggios of grape essence in your brain.
A bullhorn blurts your vanilla-flavored
name and two policemen made of incense
apply bright handcuffs that render you mute.

Dream at the Public Library

In the farthest corner of the old brick building
a starved boy reads a ruined book, tearing
pages from the spine. They turn to ash
in his hands. You realize this is you, many
years ago, the tousled blond hair and
stained shirt, the intensity that banished bullies,
the parrot on your shoulder when you read
Treasure Island, and the hovering curses you
tried on the nuns, that led to painful punishments.
Reference books did not record your past
and so you write it down, hoping only the
secrets fade. A man drowning in encyclopedias
gasps and cries *As knowledge accumulates,*
knowledge is lost! You walk the stacks,
fluorescent light basting you in silence.
Some books shriek when you pull them
down from the shelves while others open
onto emptiness, mausoleum scent wafting.
Plate glass windows look out upon a lawn
where maniacs march with protest signs,
insisting everything must burn to purify
this public place. You approach and ask their
leashed children if they might like a story.
Machine guns open fire. *Wait,* you cry,
let me explain! You open your shirt and your
abdomen, a screen, shows footage of peasants
clawing potatoes from muck. The crowd
goes catatonic, giving you time to escape.

Cactus Dreams

1. Dream in the Canyon

Without warning, the earth opens,
swallows the trail ahead.
You approach the edge of
negative space where high desert
once ran toward morning but now
yawns, a chasm not easily crossed.
A hawk circles overhead, cries the
name you were given when you were
still a thief living in shallow caves,
dashing your brains on starlight,
befriending cougar and bear.
Your feet descend without permission
past bands of cream and scarlet rock.
Ribbons of sparkling grey bespeak
compressed generations, a billion
cycles of sun, rain, flood, drought.
When you stop to rest, canyon wrens
alight on your shoulders. One whispers
convincingly that you can fly.
You test new-feathered arms above
the green, snaking river, aware
this journey will take some time.

2. Dream Among Saguaro

Distant slopes bristle with forked figures
that undulate in rising heat, trunks
thick as a man's torso. You ride a huge
sorrel horse, on loan from an old
Western. When you wish for spurs
they materialize, strapped to your bare heels.

An Apache man steps from behind
ponderosa pines, grins and fires a shot
that painlessly pierces your cheek.
Then he turns into a sandstone pillar.
Your horse is now a hawk and you must
clutch fistfuls of feathers as it rises up
a thermal. Far below, a fleet of RVs flees a
burning metropolis, all the gasoline gone.
Your raptor alights atop an organ pipe.
You reach between spines to stroke
the ridged green flesh and another limb
recoils, ready to strike. Faint voices evoke
lost centuries of wind blowing moonlight
cool across tortured contours. A chorus
of diamondback rattles resounds. Lightning
splits a rock and sulfurous plumes ignite.
Your skin has toughened in the sun.
You raise your arms just so and become
one with the denizens of this arroyo.

3. Dream on the Mesa

You climb all day and yet the rim
recedes, a green lie told to the slope by
buzzards summoning thunder from
anvil clouds, urging all creatures to
become carrion. Rufous hummingbirds hover,
red and gold sprites in hot air perfumed by
juniper and piñon, tendril tongues flicking
in the groins of blooms, lapping up
from your ear sugared words left by lovers.
Prickly pear wrestle among rocks and
shed skins of gargoyles stationed here
to guard the curve of an ochre river
choking on adobe dust, curving round
bluffs, gouging cutbanks. At your footfall,

arrowheads burrow into dirt, the shafts that
bore them toward bounding deer
decayed into dust millennia ago,
as are the hands that stretched the bow.
Your boots dislodge a sandstone slab
that tilted in place for centuries. Coyotes
in the canyon cannot forgive the coarse
song of the boulder's descent, tumbling
music scraped off the earth, and so will
snicker all night from behind thick stands
of cholla along the ravine, whose spines
stab the dark and draw ghost blood,
garnet beads glinting on moonlit rocks.

Dream at Chartres Cathedral

You stand in the chilly nave, neck craned,
glass scattering a blaze of colors over stone.
The benevolent lady with bright blue halo
frowns an hour but the instant you glance
toward the chancel her countenance shifts
to a thin smile, animating a thousand
dazzling figures. A headsman slashes a
saint's head off his shoulders and bowmen
fill a bound body with arrows. Supplicants
writhe beneath a throne as dozens of Christs
are nailed up at various Golgothas,
though always by the same angry thugs.
At a side altar, a Hebrew priest plies his
circumcision knife and a puny Jesus wails.
Zodiac denizens awaken, a Capricorn
goat-fish swishing scaly tail and bleating,
Aquarius spilling water from his amphora.
Taurus breaks free of his stone pane,
rampages through the cathedral gift shop,
wrecking racks of figurines and faux relics.
Mary keeps smiling, though for centuries
her babe has squirmed, tired of each sunrise
illuminating scenes of his pending crucifixion.
From somewhere above comes the sound of
hammer on chisel and you follow the echo
to a dim alcove where an ancient mason
carves in a shadow his lost lover's face.

Dream of the Skydive

The plane is cramped, thin fuselage full of jokers
and gods, people in costumes you nearly recognize,
their pupils spinning. The craft climbs quickly,
horizons tilting at odd angles, effervescent
clouds streaming in and out of view. The humor
among passengers grows grim, the laughter thin
as watered milk, and there's a hand on your thigh
but no way to tell whose it is. The hatch
flies open and in comes the knowledge
you must return to earth through this portal.
No one makes eye contact. No one wishes to hear
the sins of anyone else, nor the excuses.
You have never been so close to birds
and yet so far from their form. Your turn comes.
It is best not to hesitate before entering
icy water but emptiness is different, atmosphere
foreign without a margin of solidity, a far shore
to swim toward. The leap is not of faith.
You accelerate in seconds, spread-eagled,
crucified by tremendous wind. Your lungs,
useless as flat tires, quiver in your chest.
The concept of up is an enigma and down
is different now, will never be the same.
You surrender to an enemy, the first time
ever, and the pond below becomes a larger lake.
Free fall finished, you reach and grasp the cord.
It is best not to hesitate when approaching
packed dirt at this speed. You tug and shoulders
open into wings, jolting you nearly awake.
Loose shoes fly from your feet, spiral away,
messages in bottles sailing toward a
field full of spectators who cannot rescue you.
The peace, the silence and the peace, overwhelm.

Men were not meant to fly, you realize this
now more than ever. Suddenly, a bowl of peaches
seems like the best meal. You yearn
to land and lie long in deep green grass.
Friends wait at the circus tent, dispassionate cameras
ready to record either splat or smooth descent,
their upturned faces gazing past you to the
bright and flapping fabric of your chute.

Dream of the Bad Motel

The highway to this town traverses
mountain passes desolate as Pluto,
plunging along an angry river swollen
by May melt, rocks concussing in
muddy swirls and pine trees, roots
skyward, lurching over falls.
At some blind curves, roadkill rises,
shredded and bloody, to dart across
both lanes and die again
beneath your wheels. At the diner
your hands shake so bad, coffee
forms a puddle on the counter
and your reflection there is
a death mask, eyes pinched shut
to prevent final darkness from entering.
Next door, a rusted sign's neon pulses
Vacancy as if it means your life.
A malevolent row of low sheds
materializes within a bloom of dust,
doors not numbered except for the last,
half-open and spilling gloom.
The drunk clerk is mute, handing over
the key as though saying goodbye.
Of course, your room is the one
you'd feared. The maid toils there,
tattooed like a circus freak and reeking
of ammonia, tobacco, too much
lavender perfume. She grunts, tucking
fitted sheets over corners too late to hide
the rank mattress stained with a face
familiar but beyond your recall.
The carpet writhes beneath your shoes
like a nest of termites. In place of a window
is a painting of a window, the scene

depicting Chivington riding down
Cheyenne children into the dirt. The TV
works but plays only stations
from the Springs, ersatz preachers
discussing sodomy and marketing strategies.
In place of a bathroom mirror,
a hole is punched through to the next room,
where a trucker and a hooker . . . anyway,
you try to fall asleep. The sheets
feel like skin, pillows lumpy as a
ribcage. In your dream, you ride a
glass elevator up to a penthouse
smelling of mint and vanilla,
but that is a dream within a dream,
which cannot last. Trucks rumble past
all night, shaking loose plaster and
waking the rats. When morning comes,
you find your hair has turned grey.

Dream on the Underground

A woman stands next to you in a dingy train,
her face smooth and blank, just the suggestion of
eyes that stare into nothingness, a subway wall
blurring beyond smeared windows. She speaks
just one word as she reaches between her ribs
and pulls out her heart: suffering, she says,
and it detonates, tossing bodies, burning,
rending steel and shattering glass.
Ears deafened with ringing, you stumble
through smoke turned to liquid by screams,
then fall beneath trampling feet, the crazy dance
of terror rearranging your bones. Someone
lifts you, carries you out, blesses you
with a kiss, and goes back in. Far off, music
grows louder and turns to sirens, cut by
helicopter blades, radios, and rain.
The victim next to you rises, shakes off
mortality, and walks into a cleft in the
massive sycamore, leaving behind a
fist-shaped burl. Gulls descend to peck at
corpses. Your ears are bleeding and
sounds fade in, dragging little hooks across
soft tissue. Tomorrow, you will wake up
and remember the doctor probing for
fractures, burst organs, wordlessly
touring your wounds, laying on hands
so flesh mends and scars fade.
Tomorrow, you'll walk Regent Park beneath
charred magpies shrieking an ancient
withering curse. But for now, you must lie calm
on the filthy concrete, tasting your blood
and murmuring a poem to stunned squirrels,
sure this dream is not repeating, sure the dawn
is already racing toward your broken bed.

Dream at the Brewery

It appears out of nowhere, a huddle of squat
brick buildings astride a stream that wasn't there
yesterday. Fragrant smoke billows from chimneys
and stout men roll barrels up ramps one-handed,
Buddha-power emanating from big bellies.
A beautiful woman in a hop-blossom garment
greets you at the door with a half-empty mug, smiles
as if to say, *Sorry, but I couldn't wait.* A wave of roasted
malt aroma washes away memories of bad beer
you drank in begrimed bars where broken bands
played poor songs poorly. Brewer-angels float
among burnished copper tuns, arms laden with
hoses, hydrometers, thermometers, flasks,
glasses of gold liquid topped with white froth.
Strange, sonorous harmonies flow, galley grunts and
ethereal choral melodies. You abandon specific
gravity and lift off, Märzen in your mouth, flying
out of the roofless room and over barley fields
where heavy grainheads bob in the breeze.

Dream of the Surgeon

You wake at dawn, windows blown by the
force of your dreams, and dress quickly,
aware you're due at the hospital
in minutes. You freeze in the parking lot,
fingers gripping the wheel, a terror
of organs, bone, blood, and tissue
traversing your vision. Was this
what you sought, this profession of slices
and stitches, this profusion of helpless,
sleeping people whose trust in you is
a ponderous burden? Black bunting
appears beneath the windows of those
you will fail. The paperwork notes
no guarantees and they signed.
The anesthesiologist, dressed in
motley scrubs, rattles his rubber mace
in your face as you pass. The nurse
you dated last summer glares, her
brown eyes drilling holes in you
while you scrub and scrub and scrub.
The patient waits in pre-op, naked
under his thin blue smock, nervous
and scanning for exit signs. Your notes
indicate you'll remove both his disease
and his imagination, couched as they are
in the same swollen gland. When they
wheel him in, he's still awake, counting
ceiling tiles and whistling a show tune.
The dark drug washes into his brain.
His eyes roll back and it's showtime.
The scalpel they hand you is enormous,
more scimitar than knife. You open him
like he's Pandora's Box and sure enough,
red devils race from the incision

along with a hollow moan, like wind
emerging from a chthonian chasm. Hope
follows, preoccupied with insurance forms.
You reach in and find gems, bloody but
glinting, and also a nest of jays. There are
lost keys, a cell phone, a subway ticket.
The deadly growth you seek shrinks
from probing fingers until you corner it
against the ribs and avoiding its teeth,
seize it by one rubbery leg and pull. Stubborn,
it refuses so you yank with all your strength
till it pops loose, emitting a shriek that
shatters glass. The nurse pats dry
your brow, her hand firm and malicious.
Machines bleat faintly behind you as you
suture the clean wound closed.

Dream In the Alley

You wake in precisely the spot
where you fell late last night,
exhausted and reeking, friendly filth
caked on for protection and
a rumbling in your gut as though
your body were digesting itself.
Your Lexus is gone. Your Rolex,
gone. Did you ever own anything
but these hands? Look how the dirt
makes black rims beneath your nails.
You'll feed yourself with these fingers
if you can find food, the discarded rind
of a cheeseburger, a pizza crust,
a polystyrene tray weighted with a
plug of congealed lo mein. Your last
memory before sleep claimed you in the night
was a warm breeze tickling grubby beard and
slapping the flap of your cardboard bedbox
against the dumpster's grimy panel,
stirring scents you know as the perfume of
ruined existence, an organic comfort
after car exhaust and oily asphalt's tang.
But it's late April on the Front Range so
you wake with snowflakes on your cheek
and a stupid lost seagull swooping above,
keening a harsh rebuke because he
cannot land amid the trash you top,
a fleshy paperweight. Brick buildings
rise above this greasy canyon, exposed pipes
shushing as residents flush and wash.
Your last meal was days ago, when sun
draped promises over budding branches
and the peaks west of town gleamed white
until dusk poured purple hues down slopes.

What does the feral cat want, crouched
in the alcove of the shop's dented door?
You wish it was a cougar come to
eat you and thereby deliver your soul
to a special heaven reserved for those
whose bodies nourish carnivores.
Your legs are so stiff they could be
cottonwood limbs bowed with a dangerous
load of spring snow. Cars slice by, passengers
leering on their way to a clean church
high on a distant hill. Jesus saves
the regulars, but those sleeping rough must
suffer and should not reproduce.
You were once a glutton and now
what you wasted glimmers, a treasure
in retrospect, garbage you'd love now.
Every window you pass is a cruel
mirror, lying to your reflected face,
your former privileges sealed behind
glass, price tags taunting the pocket
where you once tucked a bulging wallet.
Will the Mission feed you tonight,
despite your grossness, your ongoing
neglect of the gods, your previous
failures to muster compassion?
Will the rocks along the riverbank
soften into pillows? Will the pigeons
stop shitting on your head so you can
finally fall asleep? If you lie still,
the statues of Civic Center Park may
recognize your pose and welcome you to
lie for eternity at their feet. This is but a
bad dream and you hope to wake
back in the corner office of that
glassy tower, your tie too tight,

your pants pressed to creases, your
portfolio diversified and every memory
of this night fading in morning light.

Dream of the Starving Wolf

Dusk falls late in high summer, light lingering
as fir and pine melt into one great curtain of
green-black, tall cliffs softening until
you're sure you could have climbed them.
You've walked miles and come, finally,
to the pass. West lie lands so lush you will
die with that image beckoning.
Lullabies bloom when wind licks the lake
nestled among boulders below. It's peace
as you imagined it, all things you deserve
but couldn't find before, emptiness
pouring down your throat into your heart.
But none may linger in dreams
past the point of recognition. Rustling
in the manzanita summons you back
and a gaunt white wolf limps from the forest,
tongue hanging, hipbones reciprocating
under a shaggy coat. She sees you and clearly
means to approach, her hunger bigger
than her fear, more pure than your pity.
All you have left from your long trek
is a bagel, which you roll across the dirt.
She takes it in her mouth as though
lifting a pup from the den, having tried
everything else, resigned at last to
eating her young. You remember hiking
clearcuts that sprawled across the drainage
just beyond sight of the highway corridor,
virgin forest reduced to slash piles, slopes
bleeding silt into streams. Every bear and cougar
was a refugee, hiding in a shrunken remnant.
The wolf, hardly nourished, raises her
scarred muzzle and howls, and you howl, too,
voices in harmony. Your eyes course, hands

42

grow claws. The trail looks dangerous,
leading toward perpetual hunger but you
lope with her into dark woods, a companion.

Dream of the Bogman

Your crime is unforgivable. All know your guilt,
though none must speak it but the priest, clutching
a bowl of grain and ash, fine bone necklace
round his neck, eyes black as caves no bat would
enter. He's the one who will cudgel you unconscious
but not dead, assuring you wake beneath a ton of
wet turf. Was life worth this? You recall warm bread
broken and steaming on a cold afternoon, laughter
in sheltered spaces, sunrise lighting triskeles and
waves you pocked into the great stone slabs.
There was your mother singing the old songs to
chase away rain on winter nights. Now, all pleasures
must end where you stand naked in the mud,
eating your last meal from a bowl full of judgment.
Never worry about what's left undone, for lacking
an actor, it vanishes from possibility. You will
speak of these things when you're unearthed,
a leathery relic uttering the language of the dead.

Dream of the Street Poet

Hunger tickles with its thin fingers the
curves of your lowest ribs as you
sit in your stone cell high up in hills,
abandoned by sun, by friends who insisted
verses never put meat on your plate
nor sweet wine in your mouth. They were
right about the first. So you must descend
the crumbling ridge, wildflowers profuse
in the groin of every gully, cool wind
licking sunburned skin, air more rich
in oxygen with each down-step you take.
Far below, a town secretes its streets
in a ravine, aspen and spruce patches
melting blue-green into the folds. It takes you
all morning to reach the valley floor,
clutching your scraps of paper,
your stubby pencil, your perforated
sack of tales called a heart.
A gentle mutt approaches to nuzzle
your open palm and lead you to a stream
where you sip intoxicating water, clear
as your first revelation. There are many things
you need—food, bliss, the understanding
brown eyes of a beautiful girl, the touch
of another human being who has been
to the place you visit in dreams like this.
Main street smells like Hades might, exhaust
from lumbering trucks a rising murk,
but you seat yourself at an intersection,
traffic and pedestrians yielding a wide berth.
Your first croak sounds like a caw.
You remember your friends the crows
so far away so you sing instead as though
auditioning for the role of Orpheus.

It doesn't take long; across lanes of traffic
comes a woman in flowing gown, hair
dangling in long curls, lips mouthing
some kind of prayer. She opens her arms
and embraces you. *Do you have a love poem*
she asks, her voice comprised of
rills over rocks, pinecones landing on moss.
It's the one thing you've forgotten to write
up there in your eyrie but you'd rather
leap from a cliff than deny her so you
improvise, make language stroke
her shoulder, cheek, the lids of her eyes.
She sways and smiles, whispers,
This is why I came to earth, leaving stars behind.
Your poem lasts a long, long time.
When it's over, she takes you by the hand
and leads you to a shady glen where she
feeds you wild plums and bread
made from her body. You gain the strength
to climb again for home.

Dream at Bill Cody's Bar

He could be a cliché, this man beneath the black Stetson,
jawing with another poke about the gelding he sold
to *that damn fool woman*. You followed a Cody impersonator
into the Hotel Irma hoping to steal his phony goatee
but he's nowhere in view and now you're the only man
not sealed in denim and shoed in narrow boots, the only one
not suspicious of a stranger wearing the wrong face.
You wish red mud caked your city shoes and a drawl
drenched your tongue, though a handlebar moustache and
leathered skin would be too much. Surely, you'd be lost
in the local canyon before you first felt thirst.
A legless man on a headless horse materializes
out of dust blown in from Yellowstone. The barmaid
knows him well and sets down a brimming shotglass
before he can utter a word. On cue, a fierce gust
pours down the vacant street outside, rattling
riverrock set in the building's walls. Beer bottles sweat
on the cherrywood bar where cold men weep over
buffalo-bereft plains and women far too tough to kiss.
Suspicious pronghorn drink in the corner, summoning
enough courage to charge an unsuspecting local and
hook his ass with their cruel, curved antlers.
You order a steak. The surly waitress scowls,
hands you a hammer and points to a bison
tethered to a brass banister. *Try not to make a big mess*,
she says, cracking a smile marked by missing teeth.
Everyone turns to watch since it's what passes for
entertainment in this town, the braining and gutting
of beasts by visiting poets. The tool in your hand
turns into a pen and you sign the animal's hide.
You want to love these people, their languid pace, the
closed-off openness, the lithe bodies set at a lean that
requires stiff wind to push them up straight.

Your attempt to embrace the nearest one
goes poorly so you pay your check with a sonnet,
inexpertly composed. Your tip—a Shoshone curse.

Dream at the Middle School

You're a kid again in sweaty sneakers
and bad haircut, in a puny body mostly bones.
Your seat is always the same—
between two bullies who will beat you
if they catch you at recess, knuckling
your headlocked skull until knobs rise
and you drool spittle and blood
to the playground dirt. But no tears, no,
never that. The teacher is tired, her voice
underwater radio static, eyes vacant as a
dead bird's, hands trembling so badly
her chalk lines squiggle across the board.
Bells puncture boredom all morning,
often just as she's speaking the answer
you've waited so long to hear,
and then time resets, clock ticking back
to the start of the day, each conversation
repeating, again the incessant scritching
behind you as the doodling kid draws
his bizarre creatures. The delicate girl
in the front row, whose black hair is a
warm pool where you would submerge,
turns to stone when she stares in the
face of truth and now she'll never return
to childhood, that green glen where
salamanders scurry beneath slick rocks,
where taffy and soda and Italian ices
wait beyond the doors of summer,
the place you feel your mother's embrace,
your father's coarse hand in your hair.

Dream of the Headache

You wake broken at 4:15, a forsaken hour
when all that must be done awaits the
animation of your flesh and bone machine.
But rising early cheats the night, steals a day
from the end of your life to place it here.
You were dreaming of driving a
monstrous combine over a flaxen field,
the combustion engine gargling fiercely
beneath your seat, spindle blades thrashing,
thrashing down grain that a steel spider
apparatus seizes, swallows, binds in bales.
The clock ticks and your cranium becomes
a bale wrapped too tightly in cruel wire.
At first, you lie still and savor the pain
so you can name it and know it, chart
each place the pike strikes, measure
the intervals between the throbs.
When you stand, black curtains advance
from periphery left and right and feet float
on slick, warm mud, tinnitus rising with the
weightlessness. When you shake your head,
a calendar falls out one ear, red slashes
through dates, scrawled notes you recall
with a nauseous wince. Jaw muscles quiver
and your mouth snaps open, emitting a blast
of black smoke, acrid and sulfurous, remains
of a conversation where you should have
stood your ground. Small horns protrude
from your forehead, tips red hot. The damned
Sandman didn't drop granules in your eyes, he
blasted their surfaces bare of regrets
burned there like old daguerreotypes.
At the sink, you swallow a handful of relief,
knowing you don't deserve rest. Colors

lance through the dark room, strains of
bombastic music trailing. The sun won't rise
for an hour so the moon keeps pulling at the
roots of your hair, November chill stiffening
extremities as a futile furnace lights and cycles.

Dream at the Drive-In

Cars rise between speaker poles spaced like
military tombstones in pink and grey twilight.
Deep, distant voices of gods whisper
from everywhere at once, hawking
fresh popcorn and fluorescent soda,
ice cream injected with air and chemicals.
Bats swoop above the polluted Platte,
gorging on giant mosquitoes. You navigate
hilly terrain and end up parked next to a
drunk in a rustbucket Dodge sedan
who will rock his ugly girlfriend once an hour.
Dry August grasses spice a breeze.
The great screen leans a little left,
the pockmarked slate a bright cleft
among surging American elms. Once,
when you were young, there was no end
to summer and the girls you touched left
laughter and cinnamon behind.
One pushed her delicate tongue into
your mouth, deposited a map to her house.
You swallowed and it became
knowledge in your cells, a route you could
crawl in your sleep, and you did until
you became a thing nocturnal, a spider
awakening at dusk, dangling outside
her bedroom window screen, drinking the
scent of her skin. Suddenly, darkness
obfuscates your reminiscence, claims
the corrugated acre and faint light flickers
on the enormous panel, a chocolate bar
large as a submarine and cotton candy
grotesque enough to gag a giant.
The snack bar disgorges a foreign army,
men in strange uniforms, weapons borrowed

from a cruel empire, scimitars, lasers, and
night-vision goggles. A phalanx of
priests and politicians follows at the rear.
Fortunately, the projector stalls. When the
broad beam of light comes back, the movie
has begun, a scene of a man smoking opium
in a dim room, attended by a crone so small
she might be a child or a bad fairy.
Then you realize the man on the couch
is you, wearing your face of sleep.

Wilderness Dreams

1. Dream on the Peak

You stand on a boulder big as a barn,
dawn surging slow and relentless,
pink to orange to yellow light climbing
stone ladders, firing patterns in lichen
that appear as familiar faces. There are
no clouds above, just paintings of clouds,
and a raptor screeches in the voice of a
woman scolding wind for eroding rock.
You begin your ascent, dust blooming
at each step. Marmots chitter warnings from
perches in the sun and at the sound,
great pines twist and sink new roots
into rocky soil. The summit recedes.
At every switchback you kneel to
pray at altars reduced to rubble.
From the maw of a mineshaft comes
weeping and laughter, or a sound
that is both. You must lie down and rest.
As soon as you grow still, birds land
and make nests in your hair. You realize
you're on the peak, and always were.
A chill rain wets your upturned face,
glazes eyelids, salts your tongue. One
at a time, magnetic stars
pull small hatreds from your heart.
You bleed music, a piano's notes,
a soprano's highest tones. You're home.

2. Dream on the River

You wake already ankle deep, the water
cold enough to squeeze vertebra loose
and turn toes to stone. You don't advance
but the river rises around you, up, up
your calves to your knees, scarred by
chapel floors in early years, to thighs
that quiver as though this frigid stream
were one of your mistakes come back.
The river keeps rising and your testicles
leap with the shock. Currents swirl
around your waist, counting ribs.
Against your will, your arms rise
like wings, as if keeping them dry
might save you. You don't fear the cutthroat
that pluck at your navel until one
catches a thread and swims away,
unraveling lost lines of poetry,
now grown mellifluous in cadence with
water lapping at riverbank rocks
and gurgling over shallows, strumming
exposed roots of cottonwood, tuned to
wind that plays the willows and pines.

3. Dream on the Lake

A breeze of bitter pine finds your
tiny canoe, pulls you further out
than you want to go, through whitecaps
topping the deep, black water.
A great wave drenches you, rocks
the craft sideways into a trough
and a chorus of crows scream
as your boat dumps you into
green murk, the sun in the sky a jewel.

You wish you were a cuthroat, swallowing
lakewater to survive, exploring
the mossy sands by starlight, but
all too soon, breathing matters again
and you must surface. The shore is far,
a bank of blessed soil. You cling
to a gunwale as your boat drifts
and then a sandbar snags your toe.
You drag the craft ashore.
An empty dancehall appears behind
thick stands of lodgepole pine.
A woman beckons from the steps,
her face pale as aspen bark. Time is passing,
she says, and then she's gone. Your feet
chilled and dredged in sand, will not
do what you ask. Storm clouds
pour over the western pass. The lake
goes glassy. This is your chance to
push off again, paddle for the far shore.

Dream in the Tunnels of Telluride

Underground, you see the dangling legs of
lynched men, the roots of condominiums,
dripping silver back into the earth.
Phantom ore crushers pound incessantly,
piston strokes reverberating, the town
a drum beaten by demons. You knew
upon entering that you would get lost
and it soon comes true. Perhaps some day
they'll display your skeleton in a dusty
museum case, curled like a fetus, bones
in their final contortion. Still, you've come
to this canyon to learn what mines
can tell you, so willing to descend into
dark halls where black water trickles
down bare rock and dead men bang
glittering walls with hammers of smoke.
They grimace. They have no eyes.
You sing to cheer yourself and a chorus
joins in, basso profundo, tenors and baritones.
A door appears in the stone, brass knob and
scuffed pine, and it opens onto a tunnel
as well lit as streets above. A woman smiles,
threads her fingers among yours, says,
What took you so long? She leads you along
an underground lane, past heaps of
rotting snow, past a man on a unicycle,
past an old whorehouse that's a bakery now
and an old bakery that's a boutique.
You know you're still in some awful tunnel,
hallucinating like a madman and
nowhere near to waking. The ghosts begin
calling out your name. A weightless hammer
materializes in your sweaty hand.

Dream at Dun Eochla

You're the third son of a third son, posted to
Aranmore's lesser cashel, a high stone ring
atop a karstfield with a view of far Connemara.
Your job is to watch the north approach, a slope
of broken rock that clots into a cheval de frise
at battlement's base, to sound the alarm if raiders
appear in their vessels, rowing toward a landing
on the beach where harbor seals bask. Nothing
crosses the horizon, nor has anything but a
legion of gannets for a lifetime of days.
Just as you feel yourself drifting toward sleep,
two women appear, one with an axe, the other
with a wineskin. Nothing in your little stone book
has prepared you for this. The dangerous one
wants a kiss but won't put down her weapon.
Her mouth is salty and warm, her grip iron
on your arm. You plead for a sip of wine.
Oh, this isn't wine, the other one says, dangling
the empty bladder. We need a little something for the
ceremony. She smiles and you hear the axe sing.

Dream at the Harassment Training Session

The first thing you're told by the speaker is
you're already guilty. The only question is
how severe your reprimand will be.
You're directed to turn to page four
in your manual to review the list of
prohibited behaviors—no licking the necks
of unsuspecting staff, no self-immolation
at meetings to symbolize unrequited love,
and surely no use of the word *desire*
unless in the context of money or power,
for which regular orgies are scheduled.
A faint asterisk near the paragraph on
policies regarding fraternization
directs you to fine print: *these rules apply*
only to plebeians; the bosses will screw
whomever they like, including you.
The training video begins. The perpetrator
has your name and a bad toupee.
His jokes all begin in bars and end
not with sex but with punch lines wherein
candy figures large. You cannot understand
why your co-workers wear bikinis yet
take offense to the coffee-room calendar
depicting women in bikinis. While you watch,
your office mate, a woman with bad teeth
who sweats profusely, runs her hand up
your thigh, then screams and files a complaint.
In the commotion, you duck through a door
and find yourself *inside* the training video,
mouthing lines you never would speak,
aware your role in the scandal is central.
You're told to strip and report to the
office manager, who upon examining
your assets, gives you an enormous raise.

Dream on Santa Fe Boulevard

The street turns to dust, buildings to brick
and dry-rotted wood, cars to buckboard wagons.
A monster truck, stereo blasting, simply
disappears. Turkey vultures circle beneath
jets' contrails in the stratosphere. You think
the parking meters will be next, morphing to
hitching posts, but they remain. A woman on a
donkey checks them, stuffs tickets into saddlebags.
In the alley, an ugly hombre empties his bladder of
bad whiskey and glares at your quizzical look,
fingering his holstered cell phone as if to
draw it and call you at any moment, one quick
ringtone to the chest. You move on past, aware
you now wear a sheriff's star. Woodsmoke
infuses the spring twilight, besmirching the last
gold rays from a slanting sun. The murky Platte
murmurs, banks bright with shopping carts and plastic.
Vague shapes roil in the clouds above peaks
and you realize why they stopped their horses here.
A buffalo soldier saunters past, leading a buffalo.
On his heels, a punk, all ink and chrome studs,
sets off laughter like wildfires all down the street.

Dream On the Burning Mountain

When the first flames blister your feet you know
this dream is different. There will be another time
to wake again beside a cool stream trickling over
moss and slick rock, firs soughing and yielding
to breezes. You hear wicked cackling, the witch's
hilarity as she flees down the slope, crowns exploding,
spraying hot sap, ash falling in a dark caress atop
glowing brush. Thunder mocks the canyons, having
flicked its match into tinder and slid toward the plains.
On this mountain you married a girl who wove
gentian and paintbrush into auburn tresses,
the very flowers sure to emerge first among
scorched boulders when summer comes. Cuthroat
huddle under a cutbank, safe until the stream
chokes with next May's runoff of cinders and silt.
Conflagrations whip orange into night sky, sigils
leaping slope to slope, cleansing inclines of crude
cabins and mansions without discretion. The road
a bubbling black river, winds over a crest. Clearcuts
loggers hid behind ridges will flaunt their green scabs
in the morning. Futile slurry bombers disgorge
clouds of rusty dust and helicopters heft great buckets
of North Platte water that evaporates when released.
You walk in the wake of flames, feet now scorched
beyond sensation, stalking the blackened carcasses
of marmots and mule deer, smelling the scorched
bark of ponderosa pine and tasting a charred past.

Dream of the Dying Soldier

You know as soon as the bomb explodes
that you'll never lie again on grass in your
father's back yard on a warm June night,
stroking that faithful old dog and
listening to bad pop music spilling from the
window of your sister's room. Bright flames
sear your eyes shut and an oceanic roar seals
both ears. In such silence and darkness,
the faces of children surface, a boy
who chased after your patrol that first day,
until he turned into a sparrow hawk and flew
high above dusty alleys where you now hover
watching a frantic medic holding your
guts together with his bare hands.
You want to tell him it's OK, he can
just let you go, but your whispering lips
won't form the words you want. When he
starts to weep, you want to comfort him
but one arm won't respond and the other is
over there. What was the name
of the first girl you kissed and wasn't it
really about her sister's glossy black hair?
You wish the column of smoke, the smell of
burning oil, would turn into chocolate
and it does. Maybe any minute, seventy
dewy-eyed virgins will pile out of that
burnt Humvee, readying a litter for your trip.
You try to remember your absentee ballot
and whether you checked the box marked
Crusade. Look, there's Muldoon, lost
on his last day in country and he's
coming toward you, smiling.

Dream of Three Romantics

1. At Tintern Abbey

You drive at dusk on winding roads
crowded with sleek sedans, drivers frantic.
Light rain paints grey stones to a sheen
and a falcon patrols purple clouds
washing the Wye. You park but hesitate to
tread on lawns so green, skirts that lead to
crumbled stairs and gaping walls, cracked angles,
arched portals yawning at another dusk
illuminating lost panels of stained glass.
Then you see him seated on a mossy
bench, walking stick leaned against
a fractured pedestal, face screwed up as he
scribbles in a commonplace book.
He beckons you to sit beside him.
Wordsworth, he says, extending his hand,
though at times the name's a joke.
His fine leather boots are soft from
miles of trails, hills and dales, from
wandering lonely as a cloud. He indicates
ghost monks floating down cloister aisles
lugging armloads of books, linens, casks.
You sit together as twilight fades,
watch specters transpire from pillars,
seep from the creases of fan vaults,
pour from the mouths of grotesques.
A spectral chant rises, reverberates
in the ruined nave and the flanks of the
woods, dense yew and hazel, shiver.
You want to ask if that is the slow, sad
music of humanity, but he's already
transcribed that phrase before your
tongue obeys. He rises, retrieves his stick

and hat, and dons his coat. His gaze
flashes across river and wooded ravine.
A few miles above here is a splendid spot
to contemplate, and I have lines to write.
He bows and steps away, fading slowly
as he crosses the water and ascends the far slope
toward a quarter moon set in a blue dome.

2. In Bath

Seagulls whirl above the Avon's
beige flow, their wings crooked.
The sun that warmed you after noon's
misty rain lies down behind
the Abbey's gothic spires. A girl
on a flaming Vespa zips past,
her hair also afire, her voice
a stiletto in your ear. The houses'
limestone facades leak age,
brown beards hanging from
window ledges. Jane Austen's ghost
hides behind bushes in Parade Park,
stray curls dangling from her brow.
Roman soldiers huddle by an oak,
wondering how June could be so cold
while Saxon workmen pitch earth
from a ditch onto a rampart.
Keats shows up, pale and consumptive,
coughs violently and offers to
buy you a pint. What fool would refuse?
He sips his delicately, hands almost
feminine on the sweating glass,
and starts when bells chime the hour.
He checks his mobile phone
for incoming calls, sighs and says,
Oh, to be lovely and too young to die

in a city such as this. He's half
your age, a ghost fixed at the
nadir of his untimely demise. You know
his poems go unread by the post-
postmodernists, who won't embrace
the ringing song of a bronze adze
on bluestone, the chants of ancients
walking avenues over the hills. Keats
gets slowly and deeply drunk, small comfort,
and you wish you could offer more
as he quaffs the dregs, stumbles away,
gulls shrieking and fleeing.

3. In Felpham, by the Sea

On a cool morning, sea mist licking
stained cottages on a Felpham lane,
Blake strides down the track, oblivious
to the world, lone inhabitant of a
separate and vivid space echoing with
twined celestial voices, rich with the
sweet odors of farmers' furrows
cut deep beneath a hovering angel.
He rolls, ambling like a sailor,
great shoulders muscled from hefting
metal plates, all the while mumbling
snippets from the Proverbs of Hell.
He's brought a basket of food to share,
coarse country bread, a hunk of cheese,
two bruised apples, a jar of milk,
cream clotted on the stoppered lip.
He hands portions to you with
blue-tinged, calloused fingers, talks of how
in his eye bright particles form the shapes
of majestic men with luminous bodies.
Yet I buy this bread with pence earned etching

other poets' pleasant heads, pewter faces
that can never be cured of illusions.
Afterwards, he pulls a lute from his satchel,
plays a song and sings in a trilling voice
weep weep. You ask about Scofield,
the drunken soldier he found lounging
in his garden. *Sure, I duckwalked him to the*
Fox Inn, for the rogue affronted my foolish pride.
Then Blake throws back his head,
trembles with a vision, scrambles
for his paper and furiously sketches
a host of seraphim and saints
streaming from a heavenly vale.
When he collapses, teeth clenched tight,
you take his head in your lap, wipe the
sweat from his broad brow, and wait.

Dream at the Faculty Meeting

It's 3:30 on a Tuesday afternoon,
your blood sugar so low faint stars
spark at the edge of vision and
tinnitus singes your inner ear,
an ambulance wailing as it
carries away your brain.
The room is dim as the
belly of a mothballed ship,
a bilge of bad judgments
stinking and slopping the walls.
Around the table, the cast of an old
horror show gathers, reeking of
mission statements, toting data
printed on long, long, long, long
sheets. At the head, a mosquito
woman rests her bent proboscis
in a book. She's nervous, she
denies sucking blood, though her
stained face gives her away.
Next to her a gorgon frowns and
picks her teeth with a fine bone, noxious
smoke drifting from manicured nails.
Her snakes hiss and undulate,
but even that is not enough to wake
the adjacent catatonic man.
When she speaks the clock stops,
then begins its backward trek.
You wonder with a grimace whether
suicide can be accomplished with a pen.
Suddenly they're staring at you, these
zombie colleagues. Half of them have
their hands in the air and you realize
it's a vote. They wait. You don't care
and so you raise your hand. Jaws

drop and debate breaks out, rubber
swords yanked from scabbards marked
Plato, Marx, Jesus Christ Corp.
The bludgeoning begins and you duck
beneath the table, find yourself among
ancient scholars huddled and scared.
We've been here for years, one says.
You can join us if you like but please,
don't bring up new agenda items.
The noise above subsides but no one
wants to raise his head and check.
You retrieve your notebook
in the hope you can do some work.

Dream of the Alcoholic

You wake one morning and your hands are
not at the ends of your arms, though you hear them
paddling downstairs toward the cabinet. Too bad—
without them you can't hoist the tumbler
at your bedside, still half full of cheap bourbon,
the kind that powers spaceships on lost missions.
Next door, a man plays a cello badly,
his bow made from hair of delirium tremens.
You rise but can't find the floor at first
and so fall through your last nightmare where
two women spooned bad beer into you,
their uniforms so damned white you couldn't
discern the insignia—a glyph from a graveyard
stone. Probing needles filled veins and a voice said
never thirsty again while chants reverberated in an
ocean teeming with phosphorescent
jellyfish people, sharks, and sharp-toothed eels.
Suddenly your hands return, empty and
wringing each other as if they were angry lovers.
You're not sick, that's a lie others tell you,
those who resent your one comfort in life, the heat
radiated by a smoldering liver. Outside, July sun
bakes earth and small tornadoes thunder
over dun plains. Bruegal's *Triumph of Death*
adorns your computer screen where tidbits of
bad news dance—a terrorist who resembles you has
immolated a bus full of kids, some still burning
while they're being interviewed. You drink
as punishment a gallon of sour milk. An alarm
rings somewhere inside your deepest bones.

Dream of the Developer

You drive a huge vehicle deep into
virgin forest, snapping off saplings,
emerging on a broad mesa, great
tires tearing scars in the tundra
that will take a century to heal.
Angry raptors wheel above, shriek
names of children you've yet to sire.
Slopes of lodgepole pine sweep away
toward an azure bowl below. The clouds
rain cash. The trees are tubes of cash.
The stream smells like sweaty copper
jingling down the rocks. You don't mind
that the crew brought rifles
to play with the cougar's kittens.
In this new West, waferboard walls
make for quick condominiums.
You'll be long gone before the
frames collapse, your exodus slowed
only by the weight of loot as you
seek new lands for the next erection.

Eagle Dream

It's the loneliest road you've ever seen, rocks
creeping from fields to road's shoulder
just to glimpse your motorcycle slashing
through rain and bone-flensing wind.
Side canyons peel off toward bad jobs, days
in court, the house of a woman who
turned into an ancient demon, teeth and rage.
Overhead, a majestic raptor holds position,
then begins a wide downward arc, diving,
at a speed you cannot duplicate,
and he's heading for you, heading for you,
heading straight into your path. The collision
occurs with the force of revelation, light
blinding your eyes and visions of myriad
colorful scenes, people amassed on green lawns
chanting home the planes and tanks.
But in reality, or what you think is real,
your body is heaved off the cycle seat,
twisting a moment in air before
slamming into pavement, tendons snapping
like harp strings, organs bursting from their
silky bags, skin smearing the road. So
it's a surprise when you wake—is it days
later, months, or maybe another life?
All you know is your bones are stacked
on a ledge of rock, gleaming and wet, bright
adipose tissue stuck to the knobby ends of
knees and elbows. Your hide, patchy and torn,
is draped across the twigs of an eyrie,
spread out, palms up, the image of DaVinci's
proportional man. The wind's an anesthetic,
caressing away pain from exposed flesh,
and then he comes, his scent of clouds,
hailstones, ozone, bristlecone. His touch

is warm feather down but underneath hides
the strength to rend and shatter, and to heal.
His eye is brown and gold, moving over
your prostrate frame, the bits and pieces of you,
with a reverence you don't understand.
There are parts he will not put back: the hard knot
of black wire once lodged in your throat—
he drops it off the edge of rock. Slowly,
he fits your tibia back into sockets, nudges
clavicle and shoulder blades into alignment,
sets the metacarpals, smooth and white,
each into its place, pecks the center of your palms
with his beak to see the muscles clench, sinews
working the joints. It's slow work. All afternoon
the sun rolls in and out of bulky clouds while
you're reassembled and blood begins again to pump.
Your lips become pliant, though words are
not yet there. You now know this was necessary—
the breaking apart to scatter bad cells, to force
from hidden places the obstructing pebbles
blocking flow. One by one, he finds dark things and
jettisons each until you feel empty but whole,
keen in this new body lighter and stronger.
You can see further than ever from your perch,
across the broad valley where the snake of your destiny
wends between sage. *Go ahead*, says a voice,
you can do it. I felt you needed the wings.

New York Dreams

1. Dream in the Ramble, Central Park

A path opens in memory's wall and you enter.
Two crows perch astride the arch, nodding
when you ask *Is this the way?* A chorus
drifts from some far glen and in a descant,
wrens pin notes to soft summer noon.
Great humps of rock wear gossamer moss
in sun filtering through leafy beeches,
maples, and oaks. It's easy to imagine here
a peace that finally overcomes greed, a blue rain
that blurs new-minted bills and melts banks.
Lovers come to forget concrete, morph into
fathers and mothers beside babes in cool grass
beneath trees heavy with silence and bliss.

2. Dream on 42nd Street

From the fingertips of the motley man
brown pigeons flap toward a patch of grass,
carrying away small children.
A businessman, sweating green, stops
and splits open, skeleton tumbling
across the slate walk. Firemen appear
to hose away the guts. In a window
high above, a woman makes love
to a gargoyle. Busses are leaving forever
from the corner, each one full of soldiers.
They return to the far corner empty.
Somewhere, a voice rises in song, no words
but a melody so dire, great sycamores
slough their bark as though a veil falling
from a widow's face. Cool breezes

riffle ivy, nudging August toward autumn.
The busses keep arriving, leaving, the voice
keeps singing and the clock of your life revolves.

3. Dream at Shea Stadium

Cold bee-ah, can a bee-ah,
the vendor barks from mezzanine steps.
Ten thousand empty seats collect
bright orange sun, great muggy gulps
of summer. Multimillionaires
take the field beneath jets peeling away
from the metropolis. Bang!
a foul ball strikes a tourist's head
and fountains of blood erupt
in foreign lands. The pitcher,
fearing reprisals, refuses to hurl
a curveball, his best pitch. A pinch hitter
approaches home plate with no bat,
an enormous hot dog in his hand
instead. The game is scoreless, heading
for extra innings. The Mets
may never win again. Someone
in the cheap seats starts to weep.

Divorce Dream

You wake up one morning to find your wife
straddling your thigh with a hacksaw.
I'll need this, she says, for proof. To your relief,
she starts in on your leg. There's no pain now,
thanks to anesthesia, but it will come
roaring tomorrow. Across the room her bags
stand open: clothes and shoes but also
vials of warm salty liquid she will mail back
with instructions to open on snowy mornings
forever. Your bedside radio is off but
music still drifts from the speaker, Albinoni's
Adagio, interrupted by a distant ranting voice
you recognize as your own. Don't go,
you say, but too softly for her to hear,
and anyway, she hasn't listened for years.
One more time your eyes caress her,
flowing over her brown hair, her shoulder,
her hip, her vulva, where you pause
and remember the children's births.
Silently, the bones in your chest explode
with an ache so sublime that church bells
down the block chime softly to mark death.
The cat crouches in the corner of your room
and wills itself to turn to stone. A great wind
shivers the blue spruce and topples the car,
but she is strong and with one hand,
sets it aright, climbs in, and honks the horn.
What more can she possibly want? You rise
and hop out to the drive. I'm giving you
the keys to your life, she says. I never meant
to keep them. In her hand is a pen, a book,
a kiss, a compass, two coins, a shotglass,
and something invisible. Her other hand slips

inside your shirt, parts ribs and finds heart,
squeezes it because it has stopped. You notice
as she drives away a taillight has gone out.

Dream in the Ballybeg Dovecoat

You tread again the narrow footpath, enroute to
choose two doves for the prior's supper, fat ones fed on
waste grain, matins chants, blue gusts of salted air.
They sip, as do you, insistent rain, occasional sunlight
that pours through the corbelled dome's hole.
How they roost and coo, unwilling to acknowledge
their fate—the capture, the breaking, the plucking,
gutting, and roasting done by your gentle hands.
It's cold and wet in your poor cell, a life you chose,
as have the birds who choose containment daily.
But unlike them, your contentment didn't last. You check
each night as you lie awake—no wings yet, no wings,
no, never the wings. Sometimes you gird for the task of
wringing their necks by imagining they have laughed at you
trudging through manure, muck, and stinging nettles,
forth and back, reredorter to dovecoat to refectory,
or standing at the *laver*, unable to rinse away the
white dust of their droppings from your nostrils.
But truth is what the prior says and he says doves
lack souls, have neither humor nor dread and so they
fly back from wide grey skies, each to a dark niche,
when the whole world could be theirs. You must try,
he says, to be more like them and you know he means
God's hostage humbled, though you dream and dream of flight.

Dream of the Good Father

It's a journey from which you never return, this
trip toward death that begins with a birth, with
wild birds flying through your bedroom window
in a flash of blue feathers. During the night
you hear cries, then soft breathing, then
the voices of descendants whispering
what you were like. You wake in the morning
and begin to rebuild your wooden home
with stone. Your woman becomes a queen,
a good sorceress, a magic being you embrace
when she is an elm and your touch turns her
to a peach tree heavy with blushing fruit.
Everything around you is hungry and you
are the food. Everything that mattered
yesterday has rinsed away. Your face appears
on a small body and the hair that falls
from your head takes root again on its
new globe. You must teach this creature to
swim in murk where monsters hide. Show
your scars, sing your songs, put that broad back
to use. You'll be loved, first and last, though
in the gap between you must be denounced,
a lumbering bear from which all figures flee
though you mean no harm. Here is the place
where all this must be accomplished and
this is the time. Do what you know you must.

Dream on the Western Slope

March sun melts the mesas north of town
until they slump like neglected sundaes,
red mud puddling around the base.
Monster trucks roar down Main, fleshy bits
of old hippies stuck between tire treads.
Radio man bleats fanatical fear but
forgets to flush. You wish away eons
and the Colorado and Gunnison rise,
rush, wash away Cadillacs, campers,
pickups, sloshing through street canyons,
uprooting brick buildings before settling,
an oxbow lake, a chunky stew of wreckage.
Great beasts loll at the shore, hungry for
primeval ferns, themselves the answer for
other beasts' hunger. You sure were a
clever ape to wish for this, for a fold in
spacetime, a glimpse of after-man.
Who could have known just how temporary
we were, how pathetic our mathematics, how
foolish our rulers, how useless our prayers?
What will you do now? With whom
will you mate? Where in such a revised
western town can a guy get a good bagel?
It's too late for do-overs. Extinction is just a
ramp where we exit the carnival ride. Did you
fear you might puke when you breached
eternity at the apex, that instant when gravity
grows irrelevant? Surrender to this, or if you
must argue, argue then with fossils
who once spoke your tongue before they
lay down in mud to practice listening.

Dream at the Airport

You arrive late for your flight, suitcase
bulging with a dangerous psychosis.
Weird bald men in the lobby sell
nylon carnations with human faces and
books about imminent doom. Airplanes
arrive from Dallas, Los Angeles, Paris,
softly nosing smoky concourse glass.
Despite ubiquitous signage you have
lost your way among halls looping back
past fast food counters and gift shops where
bad magazines and novels jam shelves.
The bathroom, your last refuge, features an
attendant who wants to flush for you.
Pilots, unshaven and exhausted,
hurry past screens that read delayed ha ha.
Children drool and scream, their mothers
fierce as big cats cornered on a carpet veldt.
Your bagel and coffee costs 22 bucks,
the angry cashier crying out you're a
terrorist because you pay entirely in coins.
Suddenly, your suitcase is gone
and you pity the thief who in some
drab hotel will unpack its fear of
failure and tubes of nightmare cream.
A bell goes off and jet engines rev and whine.
You enter the first gaping gangway,
willing to board a flight that isn't yours.

Dream in Salida, Colorado

Sunrise crests the southern peaks,
strikes the white hut high on the hill,
casts shadows along a railroad spur.
Winter rode in on a boxcar last night,
spent the new moon's savings in a
ghostly brothel. All night, wind ran
cold hands up the valley's thighs,
bristling with newly naked aspen and
pines that know not the beetle hordes.
An old man with smoldering beard and
eyes of grey glass cries outside the Victoria
tomorrow and tomorrow and tomorrow
but he's more Lear than Scottish thane,
banished as he is to a mountain moor
far from daughters loyal or treacherous.
A brewpub inhabits the old mortuary,
customers soaking up suds instead of
embalming fluid. Every alley you skirt
harbors defrocked Klansmen who
scurry into dilapidated shacks or dive
into dumpsters, mumbling of nooses,
shotgun blasts and crucifix ash.
The Arkansas flows wild silver between
hot yellow cottonwoods, a river anticipating
canyon curves but regretting, like all
pure water, flowing closer to the Springs.
Look west toward Monarch Pass and see
in the flats green fumes rising from a
herd of porcine developers who dream of
bedrock, valleyview, alpineglow over
identical subdivisions, followed by the usual
quick getaway. You wish to be a trout
swimming upstream and even as you
whisper those words you wake

in clear shallows, current strong
through your gills, jeweled beams
lighting your flanks. Autumn is over
and you know in your fine bones you must
swim and swim and never stop.

The Teacher's Dream

You know it's a dream because
as you arrive at work, park the car
and walk up the steps, you see
two long lines of administrators
standing and cheering, tears
in their eyes instead of yours.
The one at the front hands you the
pay raise due ten years ago,
then kisses you on both cheeks and
as a gesture, throws himself
under a bus. You enter the classroom
to find the students seated and singing,
angelic voices praising today's lesson.
Apples, red and bright, glow
atop your desk. The principal
interrupts, apologetic, and
reaches into your file drawer,
yanking out sheet after sheet
of unfunded mandates.
The standardized tests arrive,
pages blank, and you
instruct the kids to draw
what's in their imagination.
The hole in the ceiling that
all winter long dripped
melting snow onto the
poorest child has been patched.
At lunch, cafeteria workers serve
fresh milk, new plums, veggies
crisp and delicious rather than
boiled down to mush. The children
ask for more and they get more.
After school, parents arrive for
conferences, shake your hand,

thank you for your efforts,
and not one mentions the
special treatment due her kid.
For once, your desk computer works
and you finish by 5 o'clock.
Radio news on the drive home
reports the Governor has been
replaced by one who can read
the handwriting of children.

Medical Dreams

1. Dream at the Phlebotomist's Office

You fast as directed but having
misread the directions, starve 12 days
instead of hours. When the elevator lurches,
your skull blossoms and your spirit escapes,
diffusing in September breeze. You awake in Eden
amid palm fronds and birdsong, a pool of clear water
lapping at your toes, stitches marking a long gash
in your side. A naked woman, lab coat slung
over one arm, emerges from behind a tree
that bears bright fruit. She ties a tourniquet
high up on your arm, tightens it until
your face goes numb and tiny bees start
testing your skin from inside. She taps and taps
a buried blue vein until it bulges, then slides steel
so smoothly in you think it might be love.
Instead of blood, little black letters spill out.
You hope they're random but no, they line up
into words and sentences—*I hate it when people
lie to me. Will she ever love me again? When I was
10, I killed a blackbird with my pellet gun.*
You yank the needle out of your arm before
further revelations assemble. The woman
looks you in the eye and says she understands.
She hands you a bandage made from her flesh
and kisses the top of your head, pads off
barefoot, hips swaying, brown hair a cascade.

2. Dream at the Checkup

You arrive an hour early to find
no magazines except *Modern Mercenary*.
The receptionist bears a resemblance to
Sylvia Plath, writing as she does in
couplets on your chart. She hands you a
clipboard with a thousand forms, requests
your insurance card and snickers
when your wallet spills Confederate bills,
photos of an ugly baby. You pass time
watching gurneys go by, canned music
dissolving your brain. An assistant
calls you to a private room so small
you must embrace her to enter. She smiles
and runs her tongue into your ear
but you can only say, *Not now*.
She tries to take your blood pressure
but the inflatable cuff will not
inflate. The doctor enters and announces,
without examination or trace compassion
you'll be dead in six week's time, then
introduces his good friend, a priest
from the temple you stopped attending.
He begins to recite a synopsis of your life,
lingering only to enumerate in detail
certain sins with which he is obsessed.
Surgeons' assistants whisk you away to a
bright room but refuse you anesthesia.
Luckily, the scalpels are blunt. A frustrated
physician gives up without making a cut.
Your angel shows up, the familiar one with
bad teeth and a broken wing. He suggests
the bar down the street where happy hour
is just about to start, and he offers to drive.

3. Dream at the Veterinary Hospital

On the first Friday of summer you find yourself
hefting a dying beast into your truck,
driving down the highway fast enough to
melt the left shoulder. Cumulus clouds, the thighs
of dark giants, mount and thunder east of town,
curling cottonwood leaves. A sign on the
hospital door reads *The doctor has died.*
The receptionist is too wrecked to speak, to
work the phone or keyboard. She has
borrowed her face from a woman departing
on a wretched ship for some forsaken place.
The remaining surgeon, an intern, guesses
the reason for your animal's distress but
exhausted, falls into troubled sleep and you
let her go, sure she needs that cure.
In the x-ray room, your trembling canid
becomes astronaut, sacrificed to science,
strapped into a harness in a small capsule,
g-forces rising. The ghostly panels on a
computer screen show elegant anatomy,
planets without names, canyons of
inner space. You'd like him to live
a little longer, to pass this first phase
of the final test. Today is not a good day
to die, you tell him. He responds
with the only word he knows, which is none.

Dream at Roxborough

Solstice sun warms rattlesnake dens,
waking the slim brethren too soon
and they slither forth, ephemeral streaks
over rocks dun and red. A bobcat
lurks among piñon, ears twitching
when the crows' caws resound.
In the distance, pale mansions breed
along streets, particle board baileys
atop puny mottes, drawbridges open
to disgorge or swallow trucks.
At first, this shortest day's shadows
are just swaths of lack-light
creeping east across the rampart road,
but a frigid wind signals and they
undulate, grey flames flickering
across the plains, advancing toward the
ugliest subdivision, urged on
by hawks and mumbling scrub oak,
until a dim edge of twilight
consumes the first abode, belching
sawdust and splinters, leaving elms and
blue spruce standing, stoplights blinking,
swaying above churned earth.

Dream at Stonehenge

You wake before dawn, leave behind your
cell phone and car keys, don a silly robe,
fantasy of neopagans who never
missed a meal or shivered through
long winters in a mud hut. You hoist the
antler-tipped staff into moist Wiltshire air,
all soft light and fecundity. Tall grass
threads between the avenue's stones, gleams
with dew amid a great forest of oak,
hazel, yew. Huge dolmens emerge
from the mist, lintel slabs fitted to
sarsen stones, not symmetry but something
more lovely. Then you hear it—
hammer and chisel, the unmistakable
ring of steel on stone. You rush forward,
tripping on your hem, and spot a man
on the circle's far side, his hammerstroke
cleaving a hunk off a bluestone pedestal.
Your first thought is to strangle him,
bare-handed, ritual justice for a vandal,
but you'd have to do the required dance,
the burning and burying, such a bother.
He's backed his panel van up to the spot,
the whole thing listing to one side
under its load. *I'm building a wall,*
he explains, *to contain my past.*
You utter a curse but it comes out
in a strange tongue you don't recognize.
The man keeps hammering as a
bright green bus arrives, disgorging
a contingent of chattering tourists.
The sun slips a gold lip over the horizon,

but even as the first beam strikes a slab
the disk drops away from sight. Someone
is selling ice cream. Two Harrier jets
buzz the scene. The largest stone falls,
crushing a man with his camera raised.

Dream in the Cavern

The cavemouth gapes, earth exhaling
all accumulated evils in a cloud of bats,
Mexican freetails, insect eaters, swarming
warm-blooded denizens of a shady shop
where only darkness is sold. Descend
and the cerulean maw above you shrinks
until its light is merely a weak blue hint
of the life you leave behind, a fading map of
good deeds, good intentions, failed attempts
at transcendence that led you here to a hole
in the ground. The path grows slick, the air
dank, stone silhouettes around you glow
pale hues of gold and green. Your light
is a feeble ray in blackness deep enough to
swallow the whole human history of
cruelty and ignorance, genocide, war,
silly religions whose priests dressed in white,
burned women because they carried
sachets full of herbs. Stalactites drip liquid
as they have for millennia, yearning
to meet sturdy stalagmites, corollary
pedestals that rise too slowly for measurement
yet serve as proof of powerful patience.
In clear pools never illuminated, tiny
crayfish scuttle, surviving on water, stone,
and the rare bug whose unfortunate journey
leads it here to fall, lost and exhausted,
to the puddle. This place is nothingness,
negative space, limestone temple of nihilism,
aglow only when you flash a lamp across
its damp surfaces. Speak and the cavity
murmurs back the secret names of those
you have forsaken, including yourself.
Whisper a lie in this labyrinth and listen

as it percolates up, emerging as truth in the
chill air of the Chihuahuan desert above.
You've heard echoes before but never ones
like these from gypsum tongues folded into
pastel draperies hung above bulging
jade stucco, gigantic iced cupcakes, great
phalluses forever erect in eternal grottoes.
The way back ceased to matter once you
passed the place where you hoard your
best dreams, the storehouse of this poem.

Dream in the Hyatt Hotel, Chicago

The rooms resemble caves
thirty floors up with view of the lake,
of streets below, the distance
a huge leap, though as with any hotel,
each guest must somehow leave.
All night the glass elevator rises
and descends, you the only occupant,
your dark suit suffocating though
you'll never admit it, never
cast bloodshot eyes on the tiny girl
dancing across lobby tiles, safe
for now but soon to grow up
in a city of legendary slaughterhouses,
black palaces, steaming manholes.
All night the foyer fountains boil and
bare trees outside the smoky glass
shake branches so wind won't attach.
A ghost pianist swirls the veil of a
melody so sad the escalator sags.
By the river's bridge an Illini chief
beckons to you, points out a massacre
buried beneath concrete. His grief is
real, even if he's not, rain slanting
and etching in granite his face.

Dream Beneath the Cloudburst

White hot needles flick fire into
slopes of beetle-killed pines and
clouds split, empty a whole year's
reservoir, hail hammering,
flattening crops, shredding
the green tent of woods. Your car
hydroplanes, and then becomes a
canoe in a river not meant for rafts.
You paddle madly, affecting nothing
in a muddy gully gushing with
snapped limbs, brown foam,
a frightened cow, a rusty
pickup, a lost country's best tools.
The rain is gasoline. The boys
are coming home. A train rolls by,
impervious to the slashing storm,
derails on purpose and keeps going,
over the far grey hills. The deluge
increases until everything floats.
Downtown, towers unplug from
cement and roll like logs
in a flume, bumping, submerging.
You're smug because your feet
are webbed—a little secret
you've never told a soul
but now you're glad as you
swim with the current, dodge
debris, wait for the torrent to
tail off, hoping high ground
will soon appear so you can
some day tell this story in a
desert cantina with the sun
shining bright in your eyes.

Dream of Raptors and Scavengers

You want out of this dream
as soon as it begins in the
winter-darkened room where
violence overtakes your sleep and
shrieking gulls peck a dead dawn
into bloody shreds. There are
voices behind trees and trees with
voices of their own, all saying *wake*,
and you definitely would, but
here it comes again, the owl
with a small rabbit in her beak,
the flesh that will feed her young.
You're lost in a world of predators,
even as fading starlight pierces
drapes that stir but don't part.
You're sorry about something,
whatever it was, and say so, but
in this dream you can never recall
just what you have done.
You struggle awake, falling into
your woman's embrace and she
kisses you until you stop shivering,
kisses you into consciousness.

Domestic Dreams

1. Dream in the Back Yard

The dog gnaws an enormous stick,
a joy only animals know
glistening at each whisker's tip.
Though it's only April, corn stands
shoulder high, stalks green
as an elf's tongue, bulbous ears
budding below tufted silks.
Two neighborhood children pass,
giggling, then unfold their wings
and fly off, magpies by the time they
perch high in the enormous ash.
Honeybees hum harmonies,
dipping into *valerian* blooms,
and dangling laden legs they
drunkenly head for the hive.
Inside, your supper cooks itself,
fragrant steam rising, as a
bottle of burgundy decants
into a glass and a wooden spoon
stirs the soup without a hand.

2. Dream on a Quiet Morning

Before quiet departs the neighborhood,
chased by the rattle of garage doors
and the low drone of invisible planes,
you open the gate with the broken latch,
step through the arbor and traverse
a cool brick walkway, sure the whispers
are silverlace leaves, not the breeze
between them. Hazy May sun

is pale and welcome, not yet the tyrant
of late summer that blazes and burns,
ripens the bulbous tomato and
swells squash into monsters.
You take the tendrils of a vine
and weave them into the trellis,
marveling at their overnight growth.
Soon, the phone will ring. Soon, a task
and then another task will crowd the
afternoon, loudly pushing to the front.
Soon, this hour will fade away, taking
the songs of birds, the damp earth,
the popping of stubborn crabgrass roots
pulled from soil. Soon all this will
turn back beneath the surface,
though your hands will be calm all day.

3. Dream of Honeybees in the Clover

While you sleep through a warm June night,
your woman and children sweat
colorful scenes into their sheets
as a crescent moon unstitches
daylight from your lack of dreams
with a sharp but benevolent tongue.
All night long, clover advances,
opening out in the moist dark its
delicate fronds and purple shafts,
three-headed creeping rootmass
driving through poor soil as
pale light burnishes plains
on its way to your porch. At dawn,
sun coaxes sweet miasmas from blooms,
summoning black and yellow engines
from hives, a pouch of pollen on
each foreleg, proboscises plunging in

nectar nooks, a sizzling mass
hovering above the expanse of turf.
You remember stepping deep into that
plush green days ago and a black stinger
lodged between your toes, tattered
flesh-end where it tore from insect abdomen.
You winced for the bee, not knowing
your leg would soon swell large as a melon.
Now you're a bloat-footed king
on a throne, high summer songs in the
throats of kids on bikes, popsicles
dripping across their wrists. Neighbor dogs
pant in a lost language, synchronous
sound hinting at secrets like the symmetry
and strength of dragonflies' wings. You drown
in this lush landscape, drinking
like the bees what is sweet, burrowing
in cool clover for a face full of perfume.

4. Dream at Lughnassadh

At first, all you hear is a murmur from the
garden's far corner, as though green tomatoes
were discussing mutiny, pressing reluctant squash
to make a choice. Soon, rustling leaves become
the sharpening of knives, the seasonal
bloodletting about to commence. Oh, for a bushel
of sleek eggplant whose thorns are soft and
don't pierce flesh. The vine is an insane woman
whose hair will not stop growing. Magpies land amid
tumbling pumpkins, their beaks seeking
mosquitoes and ladybugs. Will the fox hunt
housecats tonight or will a wash of stars
hypnotize her, spinning so wildly she is willing
to lie still under a slivered moon and forget
her pups' hunger? Rare morning rain softens dirt

in the warm dawn, dripping from all that
in summer fecundity heavily hangs.
In whispers you wonder if Lugh could explain
why we were dropped here like fruit to rot,
if not for our seed. Faces on the paper money
in your pocket bicker about the awful war.
Your questions seep into dirt the way tears
moisten a shirt. The harvest is planned
for tomorrow and already, workers gather
outside the hut, waiting for work, their
brown faces hungry, their hands tough.

Dream at Père-Lachaise

Yours is the oldest mausoleum in a forgotten quadrant
far from the graves of important persons, lying rather
among vaults last visited in a previous century.
The bent ironwork of the door shifts its shape,
sometimes depicting scenes from your life—an orgy
of disappointments, an empty landscape where
one man climbs a hill. On other tombs the bars evoke
an ornate face, horned god or demon hovering over
tortured vines violent in their interweave, leaves
wrestling other leaves. April dusk spreads
strange light and shadow over nearby marble
sarcophagi, altering the dates of birth and death
so that some who haven't yet died writhe in their
coffins under the earth and you can hear this
occasional agony. Down in the 6th Division,
the long dead rise to the surface, Morrison
a mad dervish awkwardly whirling, all the acid
in his bones giving him fierce flashbacks. Nearby,
Heloise and Abelard make mineral love atop their
canopied tomb, hands clasped so long in prayer
now free to again caress a forbidden lover's flesh.
Dead generals thread among the memorials,
saber scabbards clanging against crypts.
Painters dab invisible canvases, their brushes
dipped in a palette of pale grey pigments
while phantom poets, poring over old poems
no one will read again, scratch out imperfect lines
they might have changed when they could rise, revise.
You wonder whether such an awakening
is fair to the cremated, lithe wisps leaking from
epitaphs, ephemeral faces forming among
flowing stone tendrils. This city of the dead is an
inverted place, the soil demarcating then and now.
Your time above is short, you know. No welcome

awaits below, no acknowledgment by the restless.
Perhaps you'll lie there for millennia before
someone with a little map visits your cenotaph,
mistaking it for some celebrity's sepulcher.

Dream at the Bad Restaurant

You take your seat in the dim room,
a place that won't be here next month,
when boarded windows will announce its demise.
For now, bored waiters lean in doorways,
dream of cigarettes they want to smoke.
The hostess polishes shining spoons and
weeps black tears. You can't quite place the
awful music, nor the strange scent that wafts
from the kitchen. Paintings on the walls depict
scenes from the ongoing war, the taking of
children from mothers, the hanging of men
in a village square, poor people assembled and
weeping outside their blasted hovels.
The window you saw upon arriving
has disappeared. A grinding sound
emanates from a far table, then a shriek.
You've lost your appetite. The table rocks
and your feet tap the sticky floor. Your chair
leans to one side, ready to give way. You drink
another glass of tepid water, waiting
for someone whose name you can't recall.

Dream of the Golf Widows

The golf widows emerge from the clubhouse.
You can tell by their flaming hair and
bare breasts that this is the end.
Golf will never be the same.
The soft clicking of balls at dawn,
the spray of sand over bunker's lip
will never be the same. They charge up
curving fairways like French peasants
coming for you, a doomed prince
in pastel sweater and ridiculous spiked shoes.
You can't outrun terror, seeping like chilled dew
up your socks. The golf widows wave
long irons. No minor beating will suffice,
they mean to cripple you for life, to crack
your shoulder blades in half, whack kneecaps
and take divots from your scalp.
In their eyes you see the afterimage
of yourself, thrusting clubs into trunk,
slamming it shut and doffing your cap.
It's useless to protest. Golf widows can't appreciate
poetic plugged approach shots that drop
down to the green, bite in, draw back
as if on string, stopping a foot from the cup.
They'll never know how on the day's first putt
your ball rolls over wet grass, flipping up a tail.
You wonder: can sex be replaced
by one good drive, the struck ball hurtling
in its arc, fading, bounding, rolling into rough?
You should have taught her how to play,
insisted she attend the golf pro's clinic on
mechanics of the swing. Now your only choice
is to submit, to bow your head and pray that
in your next life you may make the tour.

Dream of the Leaving

You have chosen to leave at dawn but
dawn doesn't come. Instead, wyrd women
visit your bed to tell you a gate is opening
and you can pass through to a red stone land
where lizards will know your name.
So you rise in the dark but your shoes are gone,
and outside, summer's last cricket slows
and slows and stops. The car starts itself,
having been packed and waiting for days.
Upstairs, you have one fork, a chipped cup,
a plastic bowl, milk, and cereal so old
it has congealed into a brick. The car horn
blares. Two hot points of light begin to spin
inside your head. Who will say goodbye
to the goldfish? Who will tend the trailing vine
and fix that old broken door? Who,
in the end, ever lived here? Voices murmur
as though your goodbye party were a
collection of doubters with their purple shirts
and strange way of frowning at jokes.
You realize you loved how the light waned
through the kitchen window in winter when
afternoon gave in and let night flood streets
with cold, with dark that swallowed shadows.
Now it must be done—the shouldering of
bags and fumbling with key and lock, events
that have already happened. You must
head for the place where things are yet to be.

Dream on the Chonnacht Coast

You've been to these cliffs before, marked
land's end when maps still showed
beyond the precipice a great squid's tentacles
grappling a hapless ship. If the sun
would only shine more often here you could
forget your soggy boots, leave behind the
battered shore where wind will not cease.
Someone said no green expanse could
surpass this, and she damned with faint praise.
Wrens and blackbirds swarm you,
a wash of feathers and forlorn music
composed of departure's lone note.
You walk toward the next town where
two men greet you on a narrow bridge over
grey-green water. In their strange tongue they
name your home village, your grandfather,
who died in a far country where machines
sometimes eat men. You remember his face
from a photo, insistent eyes and a jaw that
surely felt fists. You're made a guest in a
kind stranger's house and eat your fill of
dense brown bread and fragrant chowder
flavored with sunlight and midnight both.
Come morning you awake to find
each room empty, cloaked in old dust.
Outside a woman plucks an ancient harp,
her harsh voice evoking fierce storms
that drove many fathers and sons to the deep.
Her tune loosens your forgotten past
from its mooring and it falls into tomorrow.
The ocean surges below where you stand,
again on wind-whipped cliffs, salty mist
filling your nostrils, dampening clothes.
Water roars against rocks below fields of

ruminants, stooping and chewing, unaware.
The signpost lists your destination
but doesn't state the distance yet to travel.

Dream of the Burning Man

You wake at the foot of the pyre, timbers
at random angles, a sublime construction
beyond cognition signifying things
none can grasp no matter how they stare
through tilting wood and shadow. Petrol
drips from soaked lumber, fumes
making dizzy nausea ripple up your
throat and tickle your tongue.
Suddenly, a woman in a bad pantsuit
whispers in your ear that there is simply
not enough money, and never will be,
to teach the children anything.
When she smiles, her pointed teeth
click and her makeup flakes and falls,
revealing scales. Down the hall, a girl
is being interrogated, the experts using
implements you read about in a
newspaper. You know this cannot end
well. You know someone will have to
die before the crowd will disperse, sated.
Overhead, a lone crow drops a lit match
and *whoosh*, all oxygen rushes into the
red blaze, even the little you kept
in your lungs, and with that breath goes
all the words you were waiting to say.
In the stands, a familiar face watches
your every move, and she nods as if
she knows what you will do. You climb
a nearby tree and peer into flames
to see if your name appears in licking
letters. Instead, you perceive shapes of
frightened men who hid and could not
find their way out of the woods. You
swan dive into the furnace, expecting

to burn but instead are immersed in
cool dark, a place broken promises go,
a refuge for bruised careers, an abode
of angry silence and insomnia. It's
OK. You've been there before and
are sure you know the way home.

Dream at the Convention

You approach the hotel on a
12-lane highway with no exit ramp.
Vehicles plunge off the unfinished
overpass, make perfect landings
on pavement below. You follow
but crash, then stumble into the
chrome-and-glass lobby in a
blood-soaked suit, a gash for a face.
The registration table is staffed by
circus freaks, the bearded woman and
contortionist embracing obscenely
beside a heap of swag—pens, pins,
magnets, sex toys, all in a handy bag.
They reluctantly cease grappling to
check your name, hand you a badge
that features a dead friend's name.
The program lists you as presenter of a
session that started ten minutes ago.
The topic is unknown to you.
Someone hurries up, hugs you, won't
release, keeps sobbing and asking
how you have been ever since.
You should know her voice, familiar,
surging up from memory—a rumpled
room far too warm, a woman crying
as you hurriedly tied your shoes.
Laughter erupts in a nearby hall,
followed by smoke, then screams.
You head for the bar, buy two beers,
one to guzzle, the other as a crystal ball.
You're paged on the speakers, asked to
report to a room on the 45th floor.
In the elevator, you press the only button,
a blank disc. A lurch, and then descent.

Dream in Boulder

At first you think you're in Tibet, brass head
of Ganesh the elephant god staring out through a
murky window, trunk snaking into Buddha's lap.
In the Courthouse square, a raggedy man
leaps up and dances in a circle around you,
cursing your clothes and chanting gibberish,
his puppy-on-a-dirty-string cringing with
embarrassment since he's the reincarnated
soul of a crooked stock broker condemned
to be dragged from town to town by this fool.
The bust of a Cheyenne man animates, rolls
toward a bronze soldier's pedestal, starts
whacking its forehead against the plinth until
the infantryman lifts his stone rifle and fires.
A pregnant teenager stops to give birth
and midwives materialize from every corner,
business cards flapping from pockets.
The baby emerges, spleef clenched in teeth and
dreadlocks dangling. A buffalo clatters
around the corner and runs down pedestrians,
then crashes through the café glass,
knocking over espresso machines and
scattering laptops. A gigantic truck arrives
from the Springs, roof-mounted weapons
firing. Football players drag women
through the streets by their hair. A siren
sounds somewhere as the Flatirons fall.

Dream of the Missionary

Your black suit is too small, made for a
lesser man, a boy. You have studied the script
until it colonized your brain and now
you're contagious. When first you reach
into your bag for the book, your
shoulder seam splits and foul curses
fly like demons from the gap,
shrieking truths about bruised knees of
penitents and the torture rooms of the
Inquisition, past and future, where
the real work of conversion takes place.
The natives are dark and sinful,
according to your view. Their weapons
are hoes and bone needles in a war
of sown seeds and torn clothes.
Your job is to replace these tools
with fear that is easily swallowed,
that fits into palms and pierces flesh.
The money you will make from this is
beside the point since souls
are at stake—lashed to it while you
hold the torch and pray. Your heaven is a
far place reached with wings,
from which prayers bounce back unless
the supplicant, tithe clenched between teeth,
calls out *Christ* so it sounds like *Cash*.
Your hell is this earth, blue and beautiful,
temporary but bejeweled with smooth
peaches, cool swimming holes,
a woman's thigh, a baby's wispy hair.
You knock on random doors and ask
if they've been saved and their laughter is
a signal to attack. You'll show them
what dangers lurk in failure to join.

You'll draw pictures of Satan on the crude walls of their huts so they can finally come to know both you and him.

Dream on Your Deathbed

A door slams somewhere in the house,
a crash that shudders the frame of
floors and walls. Even termites stop
and touch antennae, hoping there's
no damage to their tunnels.
From the corner of your eye you see
blue specters leaking from the closet,
people whose faces you've forgotten
floating in from distant places,
filing past the foot of your bed.
One, a woman, familiar somehow
but beyond recognition, stops
to touch your hand but doesn't smile.
It's too much. You want up, but of course
that's all over now. Your children come
and wag their heads, one weeps,
and tenderly touches your cheek
and goes too soon. You cry out,
Dinner's ready—come and get it!
remembering how they would stampede
up the stairs—but now they cannot hear
the words you have not said.
Emily Dickinson arrives with a tray
and a fly follows, buzzing
round her hair. You'll soon be there.
Paint drips from the wall and pools,
phosphorescent on the floor round a
bored priest chanting his Latin prayers,
the very thing you wanted to avoid.

Dream at Ballycrovane

A border collie greets you at the gate, trailing
garlands of kingcup and bogbean.
She won't let you pass until you pray.
You murmur fragments, incantations
salvaged from a darkened pew in the
church of your childhood, but a voice
behind the shimmering gorse says
just this once be genuine, so you kneel
among the harebells, slow your breath
to silence as wind tickles the clappers of
down-turned blooms. Willywagtails
twitter and a rook crows from an outcrop,
signaling the rusted iron latch to release
and the gate swings wide. The collie
herds you up the hill to where a
towering plinth faces high Mishkish
across Coulagh Bay, a row of distant peaks
diminishing in mist. Your fingers fit
the ogham script, millennia rushing past.
Everything synthetic vanishes—your pack,
your pants, your persona—leaving you
naked and finally in possession of
the only thing you ever had, a smooth body,
best engine ever, the big eye of your
mammalian brain open for the first time.
You can read the writing now. *Maqi,
son of Diech, descendent of Torainn,
marks this westernmost place.* At your
invocation, he rattles his bones beneath the
moss-painted soles of your feet.
Birdsong turns to chants, the holly hedge
to a procession of ancients. You make way
and one touches your cheek, leaves a mark.

Dream of the Windy Day

Dawn is still an hour off when you hear the elms
twisting above the window, scattering twigs and
birds' nests, great fibrous limbs made pliant to
bend and contort but not break. In first light
you survey the damage—heaps of red
Wyoming dirt blown south by wind,
unfamiliar cars that rock on their roofs, dazed
antelope tottering across lawns as a neighbor's
pit bull strains at his chain and froths.
A purple cloudbank hugs the foothills, pushed
along by upslope gusts. All the trash
of February skitters and leaps down the street
as if chased. You step outside to retrieve your
newspaper and are lifted off your feet,
spun round and round, grit lodging
beneath your lids and coating your teeth.
You touch down in an alley among dumpster lids
banging out a rhythm. Great glassy towers
sway all around, smoky panes shuddering
while executives stand behind them, worried
more than usual, this time about squalls,
not bucks. The gold dome of the Capitol
loosens, lifts, and shatters into
doubloons that fall, pinging on sidewalks
where a squad of street people huddle. They
leap and chase the glitter. Doors of the
legislative assembly spring open, senators
rushing out into the gale which detaches lobbyists
from their backs and blows them toward the
eighth circle of hell for a bath in boiling pitch.
The American flag tears loose from its pole
and flutters toward a far eastern land. The stadium,
built with money that might have saved lives,
rumbles, quakes, collapses spewing

bloody footballs into the sky. There is music
in the wires, a chorus of high pitch.
You hum along, sure you know the tune.

Dream in Whitecliff, Colorado

You enter on a gravel road, the only path
ever into this town. It disappears behind.
Cold air thrills your lungs and stars
spin above hunched hillsides, sifting
luminous powder into blackness.
A great cat skirts the meadow's bowl,
flanked by a river and narrow gauge rail
now a scar haunted by tough old engines
hauling ore forever toward history.
Snowdrifts grip weathered rock beneath
icicles dangling like hanged men's legs,
glinting in descending sun that retreats,
having not really tried to melt. Pines twist
in wind so fierce ubiquitous barbed wire
hums, awakens an ancient man who follows
his lost wife up the cemetery's slope,
trembling fingers reaching for her hair.
They'll find him again where he fell, frozen
but euphoric. The tavern is closed, though
through the grimy window you spy
prisoners hunched at the bar, shotglasses
full of bullets. There isn't a single bed in town
that does not point to the north. You came
because ravens called you by a secret name
all summer long, though now it's clear they
meant someone else. As you walk away,
watchers behind the drapes refuse to wave.

Dream on Glastonbury Tor

A fine mist coats the carved oak leaves
of the Green Man's stone throat,
his stuck tongue and glaring eyes
set open for centuries to watch
statues soften and rock walls fall. You walk
ancient herbarium paths, lemon balm
rank and profuse in June fecundity,
while small apples drop to the
orchard grass, emitting musical notes.
Far across a green expanse,
Guinevere walks among pillars,
her hair black enough to summon dusk
down onto noon. She beckons you toward
the hill and wrens trill goodbyes
from hiding places. The sun breaks through,
bright shafts lancing the tower,
and you see she's already halfway
up the path to the tor's top,
moving effortlessly, gold and blue gown
streaming out behind. Suddenly,
you're in armor. Its weight on your
shoulders and hips tilts you backward
on your heels. Your visor won't stay up,
keeps clanking down heavily so you
must peer through a narrow slit. A spear
bounces off your breastplate.
Who threw that? A vendor at the switchback
sells lemonade and indulgences; you pay
with a wooden credit card. An abbot's entrails
dangle from a gibbet as four men each
carry off a slab of his flesh. The lady you followed
is smoking something with an unwashed teen,
huddled around a smudge fire. The rain
increases. Somewhere below, bells chime.

Dream of the Criticaster

Having no dreams yourself, you sleep
in the same space you inhabit while awake,
a dim room where bookshelves lean
inward toward the point atop your head.
You write reviews of others' art
using only your left hand because
the right is otherwise occupied.
This is your post, guarding a
forgotten gate in a walled city
no one ever attacks. Unfounded fear
coats your tongue so you speak only
insults into mirrors you've placed
everywhere. It's fear of yourself
and the books you wrote that
no one read, though you know,
though you know, though you're sure
they were good. Your friends
have fossilized, but you still pet their
dead shapes, your fingernails
sharpened to points for the clawing-out
of eyes that see more than yours.
If your cock ever grows back it will
turn out crooked and barbed.
The asylum has the paperwork on file
and awaits only your arrival in a
newspaper coach pulled by hyenas.
For now, you will furiously opine,
bruising the fruit of all trees equally,
hacking away until the dung beetles
have finished consuming your brain.

Dream on a Hilltop, August in Iowa

Over there, you tell him, pointing out across
an endless field of corn, tassels honey brown
in yellow sun. That's where he came from
one summer morning, pushing through fronds
and screaming as if his lungs were afire.
You bathed him, cleaned moss from between
tiny pink toes, wiped the birth-grease
from the folds of his ears, rubbed alive the
tissuepaper skin of his neck and back,
kissing away the evidence of his trek.
I have to let you go, you say.
Everything beckons him away and it's best
if he doesn't witness his father weeping
alone under the oaks, a wretched old baseball
and mitt under his arm, a diminutive bat
nestling into its grassy past. You shake hands,
and when his grip releases, something inside you
gives way, a dam that will never hold back
water again. You watch him walk down a
curving path between brick buildings, hawks
pulling summer up into the sky and leaving
a warm autumn day where you stand.

Dream at the Pub

An old friend arrives, clutching his chest.
A minor coronary event, he says and
proceeds to laugh it off, tell you how once
his ex found him, naked and trembling,
on the bathroom floor and left him there
while she rummaged his desk for the
insurance policy. The waitress comes,
a woman with snakes for hair, and
patrons at nearby tables petrify
but not you two, who both know to
order beers while glancing only at her
reflection in the window. When she returns,
your friend slices off her head with his
slim cell phone shaped like a scimitar.
A winged white horse leaps from her
pooled blood. *Never mind that phony Pegasus,*
he says, and begins unraveling the tale
of his impending death, describing how
he'll step over and back, over and back
that black threshold. The effort
makes him sweat, and in sympathy you
sweat, too, trying to summon silence
in your mind but remembering how
Kerouac said death chases us
across a desert, patient and persistent.
Your meal arrives, a jambalaya floating with
forgotten faces. The band plays a familiar tune,
badly. The chalk sign behind the bar states
Happy Hour has been canceled, replaced
by a brief spell of nausea and nostalgia
for that evening when the cute girl
French-kissed you under an October sky.
Paramedics pull up and despite his protest,

defibrillate your friend until his
chest hair combusts and he's lost, smoke
rising and spelling out his will. When you're sure
he's gone, you help yourself to his beer.

Dream on the Highway, Heading South

You've traveled this road before, tires humming on
macadam a mnemonic for fear you forgot,
or wished like hell you could. Squared buttes
prod the blue belly of sky as though a painted backdrop
in a bad western where the sheriff can't keep peace
and the bad guy gets the girl. Crucifixes
keep stabbing out of soil along the frontage road,
sometimes with real gods nailed to the wood,
faces in anguish above men counting money.
The damned river flows, full of fake trout
with two heads that suck at roots of dead trees.
A factory pours its orange pigment
downstream, wretched ribbons of venom
that will twist through generations. Mansions
perch on the cliffs above town, each with its
resident vampire, teeth buried in a virgin's thigh.
The stunted forest is second growth, chewed by
pine-beetles and burned by drought. The highway is
under perpetual construction, rows of cones narrowing
lanes until trucks squash small cars or jackknife in a
spectacular spray of dirt, bone, and sparks. Roadkill
is a sport on this stretch, drivers veering wildly to
splatter rabbits, raccoons, cats, and gay men fleeing
churches of Hate under smokestacks on loan from
Polish towns, antennae transmitting digital video
Goebbels would have loved. We are not
cannibals declare the billboards, nor are we
animals. The highway patrolman is skeletal, but my,
how flashy his red and blue lights as he speeds past,
pursuing a van full of terrorists fresh from
picking bell peppers for nickels and dimes.
He calls ahead for the dungeon keeper to ready the
waterboard and branding irons. Every exit sports an
orgy of franchises, grease dribbling from vents and

stacks of boxes spilling from dumpsters. Every rest stop
has picnic tables and a shooting range, the targets all
dark-skinned faces. The sun is going down. Shadows
stretch across the road as ghosts rise, hitch rides,
and the turkey vultures circle overhead.

Dream at the City Plaza

Two stone lions
guarding the thoroughfare
step down from their
pedestals. Pale sun
refuses to cast
shadows as they lope
stiffly across brown grass
toward a woman
eating lunch. She waves
a hand with wands
for fingers and lions
turn to stone again.
Icicles rise from the
Town Hall's gutters,
impaling pigeons.
The flag lowers itself to
half-mast, signaling
another soldier was
vaporized. Ambulances
are not coming.
An ancient priest sells
indulgences from a
tent with a neon sign,
his radio playing
Spanish chants. A child
disappears inside his robe.
Suddenly, the cobblestones
rattle in their sockets
and the fountain,
dry for generations,
spurts blood and oil.
Lovers who were kissing
now tear each other's hair
and shriek. Sparrows fall

from the sky, dead.
The mayor walks past
in an ermine robe,
acknowledging nothing.

Dream in the Chlochan, Skellig Michael

You brought a cargo of sins on your leaky currach,
wondering with each dip and keel into a trough
whether you'd vomit them up, a penance for
silver mackerel to eat. Drowning is but five minutes
misery but you'll pass thirty years on this rock,
finally reduced to debating Plato with puffins
and shivering under the corbelled cap of a
stone hut, waiting for dawns that rarely warm.
Did you hate the world so much, and why?
The black-haired girl who flashed green eyes
across you cast a spell, so you pled your case.
She laughed and fled, calling another's name.
You stole a man's purse on market day, hid
trembling among the blooming gorse while they
hunted you, and opened the strings to find
you'd traded your life for a few copper coins.
Then there was the wine, always the wine
and its warm, hazy comfort until you
awoke mornings on flagstones in the square,
bruised and confused, aching and covered
in spittle and piss. They dragged you to the
stocks, threatened banishment or death,
so you lay prostrate at the abbot's feet, let them
shave a slave's mark atop your head,
and you stripped and donned a rough wool cloak
full of the last man's lice. So many years
have passed. The bells still calls at night and you
stumble up, bones aching in the damp.
The chants, at first mechanical, become
ethereal, and sometimes, whether in true spirit
or pale hallucinations you hear harmonies blend.
Then you float above it all, your past life, your
present existence on this fractured plinth,
grey rock painted white by wheeling gannets.

Dream in the Torture Room

As always, you're blindfolded, hands tied
behind your back, barefoot, trembling as they
lead you down the cold hall. Though you
cannot see, you know the room—just a chair
in the center, a drain in the floor, a bulb
dancing on a wire. You sit and wait,
weak from lack of food and water,
until consciousness floats away and you're
not there any more but rather in a green glen,
mossy rock, warm sun dappling grass,
a friend nearby humming a soft song,
so when the pipe cracks your skull it takes
a moment to remember where you are.
Your torturer speaks a strange tongue that
you ceased to decipher long ago. Once,
he wanted information. Now he only
wants to break your will, one bone at a time.
There's the smell of cigarettes and
something else burning—flesh, yours,
but the pain is a distant fire across a prairie.
Soon, the buffeting blows come and
busted lips swell, loose teeth leak blood
from disturbed sockets. *I do this
for my country*, says the man, his voice
thin as new pond ice, obscured
by the timbre of tinnitus. *You must tell me
who is responsible*, he says again, though
you have never known what he means by this.
Just say the names, he intones, *and we will
set you free*. You know he means death,
not release. You name gods and demons,
ancient poets, martyrs, messengers, but none
satisfies. *We stand for freedom*, says your
tormentor, *waging a war of terror on terror.*

My prince has exonerated me from guilt
for the things I'm doing to you.
And as he speaks, you feel his hands
searching, searching your body
for the next field of battle.

Dream at Cascade Falls

You set out on a hike amid thunder booming,
bright bolts banging against a schist edifice,
teasing the tops of beetle-killed lodgepole,
ponderosa, limber pine as big wind topples
browned sapleakers in this disaster zone.
The new hatch is coming soon, an army of
dendroctonus boring neatly out from tunneled bark
to fly for new green flesh. The shucked pelts
of pumas flank the trail, eight hundred cats
blasted by brave sportsmen who can't get
hard-ons any more, but my, they have shiny guns.
The mosquitoes here buzz by your ears,
asking permission, their feminine whispers
so desperate, you lie still while they suck whole pints,
leaving you dizzy. The mad spring creek
gushes between boulders, watersong's swift descent
a descant to trills and caws of unseen flyers.
Finally, the fall's froth appears between timber,
its roar obscuring all other sounds, the drone of
Cessnas heading for Vail, the last cries of soldiers
dying in a distant desert, the bleating denials of
a sad sockpuppet, the silence of space
embracing a warming planet. It's all you can do
not to walk to the edge of the promontory,
step off into the churn, a delicious plunge, a quick
battering and bruising, a surrendering
of this conscious life for whatever illusion
you have polished smooth all these years.

Dream Among the Lions

You huddle on the blood-soaked sand at the perfect
center of a great bowl, twelve-thousand toga-clad
patrons standing, ravenous, neck veins bulging.
Vendors hawk candy, popcorn, beer, their cries
in Latin mellifluous as a scholarly lecture, shouted.
A girl in the front row trains binoculars on you.
They've paid for this and want the close-up goreporn,
the slash and spurt, the rending of joint and bone.
Someone lifts an iron gate and starved lions
dash for the spot where you stand, their tawny skin
rippling over muscle. Your nakedness has never been more
pink and delicate. There is no question—you will
surrender to butchery. Only a few in their seats
feel the horror. You recognize none of them as friends.
Just then the lone male lion slows, mane still stiffened
from his last meal. Perhaps he's bored with easy prey
and will bat you around and leave. If not, you hope
he's quick. Loudspeakers twitch with color commentary,
eliciting roars from the crowd. Insurance salesmen
in cheap suits wave policies and pens, scream your name,
but stop short of leaping to the amphitheater's floor,
and anyway, it's too late for that. The scoreboard reads
Lions and *Lunchmeat*. A female in heat stops to mate.
You wake to find the housecat on your chest.

Dream of Counseling the Troubled Student

You begin by offering her the office chair
where many have wept or spilled their tales of
disastrous relationships, poverty, dyslexia,
all the while begging for an A.
You don't close the door, worried she might
spring a trap. You try but cannot
cross your arms or legs. You say
How can I help, making cursory marks
in the notebook on your desk. You'd prefer
a club or scimitar but stow that thought.
You look the troubled student in the eye
and nod as often as necessary, purse lips,
smile only when she shows a slight
sense of humor about herself.
At the first sign of tears you extend the
box of tissues and try not to grimace,
checking your watch when she starts
banging in self-pity as if a fly
trapped between window and screen.
For a small fee, technicians installed a button
by your desk that sounds a ringing telephone,
a rescue when all other options have failed.
You must yield or be firm, depending on
how much time remains in your career or
before your head explodes and spatters
Shakespeare's sonnets on the glass.
Firmness requires reminding her
that in South Africa, thousands of children
are dying of AIDS, that 15 species
have gone extinct since she began spewing,
a sewer pipe poised over the small lake
of your afternoon. You have, after all,
seen her burning rubber in the parking lot,
her red sports car sporting dents left by

pedestrians who failed to navigate crosswalks
quickly enough. It's a damned dilemma,
just what to do with this one, and you
ponder while she taps her long, fake nails
on a tattered volume of Yeats, leaving
bits of flesh behind. You could offer a
a make-up test, which she'd surely pass
considering the half-inch of paint on her face.
Maybe an extension or extra credit for
effort expended. Remember, it once was you
in the other chair. Did you lie? Did you beg?
Did you hate the aging professor
with his bald pate and curling nose hair, his
leaning shelf of dusty books and stacks of
yellowed lecture notes transcribed an age ago?
This much is sure: in this dream you have
removed all mirrors to assure you will not
catch a glimpse of what you've become.

Dream at Isca

You huddle in the corner of a stone cell
damp as a bog, rubbing your hands together
to banish numbness and numb your mind.
Six thousand legionnaires above you jeer,
rocking the arena as the man before you
is mauled by an angry bear. You have
drawn the wild boar, its tusks filed sharp,
flanks pricked by a dozen spears to raise
hackles, starved to hunger's frantic edge.
You check again your sandal straps, aware
there will be nowhere to run once you step onto
the oval of sand and steel gates clang shut.
You'll slay or be slain, bleed the beast dry
or be bled. The crowd quiets under
clouds scudding through a pale Welsh sky,
the silence rent only by wheeling gulls
that taunt you in words with no vowels.
Back at the barracks, a lone sentinel
regrets his post, aware he'll miss your
disemboweling. The time has come.
You rise, stamp the chill out of your shins,
don helmet, shield, and gloves. Your gut
threatens to loosen when you emerge and
cheers laud death itself, not really yours.
The beast is staked at the far rim, two men
whipping it into a frenzy. You have but a
short sword and a wish to be elsewhere,
a warm hillside with new wine in your mouth,
and the promise of her body after sundown.
Then chains slip and the mad beast sprints.

Dream at the College Graduation

A cloud of black-robed dons
parachute to the lawn, expansive
and tilting toward the far town
where a stone steeple punctures
the horizon, draws blood and the eye,
fruitlessly asserting its singular hope.
The bachelors gather, a confused knot,
square-headed and scared, vaguely aware
last Saturday's party was the last party
ever and they must now choose and
hoist a tool, wield it for 50 years.
A phlegmatic brass band blows its
lugubrious pomp and circumstance,
sweating in the hazy June heat.
Exhausted parents, released from
debtor's prison for this ceremony,
clutch cameras and hide flasks,
smiles on their harlequin masks.
The chaplain's benediction evokes
eternity, which is expected, and the
habits of hungry hawks, which is not.
Rain spatters the programs propped
in laps and someone's sister faints.
Almost heroic men rush to her aid.
The speaker is nude, which greatly
increases attentiveness. You must
all go home, she says, and prepare
for the world to end. The graduates
hurl their caps into the sky.

Dream at Carrowkeel

The last mourner, lovely daughter, rises
from her knees, from a vigil she kept on
soft turf at the entrance stone, its sinuous gap
cut for solstice sun, a tongue of flame to
coax ancestors' ashes toward another life.
Yet when she turns her back and walks away,
all that once was you sobs silently the sound
of her name, though she is deaf to this
language of the dead. The procession long since
vanished down a slope so green and fragrant
your not-body feels again a hunger pang.
This, your first dusk of eternity, softens the
edges of chamber stones, warming triskeles
that swirl under grey-green lichen, and then
even that frail light fades, a graceful sigh
toward midnight. Alone at last, bone, ash.

LaVergne, TN USA
22 June 2010
187019LV00002B/135/P